IMAGES
of America

CHELTENHAM
TOWNSHIP

Nothing better captures the tension inherent to the development of Cheltenham Township over the past century than this mid-1930s photograph of the magnificent Lynnewood Hall and its formal gardens being embraced by suburban residential development. Lynnewood Hall, albeit by far the grandest, nonetheless typified the mansions of the industrial barons who moved to Cheltenham during the latter part of the 19th century. It was said that there were more millionaires per square inch in Cheltenham than in any other place in the country. Jay Cooke, John B. Stetson, William L. Elkins, William Welsh Harrison, Peter A.B. Widener, and John Wanamaker were among this group, whose homes, built with unlimited amounts of money, became monuments to their success. However, such seemingly permanent monuments can be fleeting over time. The high cost of maintenance, taxes, and the desires of succeeding generations spelled doom for the mansions. Between 1950 and 1970, the population of the township practically doubled; thus, the vast estates were subdivided for more economical forms of housing. The development of Elkins Avenue in the mid-1930s, as captured in the upper left corner of this photograph, was the wave of the future. Although many mansions were razed, a few, like Lynnewood Hall, received a new lease on life as corporate or institutional centers. Lynnewood Hall was sold to Carl McIntire's Faith Theological Seminary in 1952, and the gardens and property began a slow decline that was highlighted most vividly in 1993 with the outright sale of statuary and interior rooms. Dr. Richard Yoon purchased the property in February 1996 at a sheriff's sale to satisfy a mortgage he held on the property. While the future status of Lynnewood Hall remains uncertain, the physical decline continues.

IMAGES
of America

CHELTENHAM
TOWNSHIP

Old York Road Historical Society

ARCADIA
PUBLISHING

Published by Arcadia Publishing
Charleston, South Carolina

Library of Congress Catalog Card Number: 2001089156

For all general information contact Arcadia Publishing at:
Telephone 843-853-2070
Fax 843-853-0044
E-mail sales@arcadiapublishing.com
For customer service and orders:
Toll-Free 1-888-313-2665

Visit us on the Internet at www.arcadiapublishing.com

The tollhouse at Church and Old York Roads was built early in the 1800s on the south side of Church Road where it is joined by the present Old York Road spur. The wagon shown here is crossing the old bridge over the Tookany Creek. There was no bridge over the creek until the county built one in 1793. The tollhouse was replaced in the late 1890s by a new building at Spring Avenue. The toll road and the Tookany Creek were defining factors in the early growth of Cheltenham Township.

CONTENTS

PREFACE

The Old York Road Historical Society celebrates its 65th anniversary with the publication of *Cheltenham Township*. This is the second book of three the society is preparing with Arcadia Publishing covering the communities of the Old York Road in eastern Montgomery County. The third book will cover the communities in Bryn Athyn, Hatboro, and Lower and Upper Moreland Townships. This book, along with the others, helps the society achieve its goals of encouraging an interest in local history and of making its collections available to the general public. The wonderful success of *Abington, Jenkintown, and Rockledge* only highlights the society's wisdom in partnering with Arcadia Publishing to make that happen.

The Old York Road Historical Society was formed in 1936 to study and perpetuate the history and folklore of the communities along and adjacent to the Old York Road from Rising Sun in Philadelphia to New Hope in Bucks County. Over the years, the historical society has offered a wide variety of programs and scholarly publications covering this area. In its collecting, the society has focused primarily on the communities in eastern Montgomery County, specifically the townships of Abington, Cheltenham, Lower Moreland, and Upper Moreland and the boroughs of Bryn Athyn, Hatboro, Jenkintown, and Rockledge.

The Old York Road Historical Society remains committed to being the best local history research facility with the best collections for the communities it serves. To this end, the society is always interested in receiving materials that relate to the local area. From photographs and postcards to business records and family manuscripts, the society is able to offer an impressive collection thanks to the generosity of those who have made donations in the past. Any additions you can make to our collections will be well cared for and most appreciated.

Please feel free to visit the Old York Road Historical Society on the lower level of the Jenkintown Library or on the web at www.jenkintown.com/oyrhs. The archive is open to the public on Monday evenings from 7 to 9 p.m., Tuesdays from 11 a.m. to 2 p.m., Wednesdays from 10 a.m. to 3 p.m., or by appointment. You may telephone us at 215-886-8590. We hope you enjoy this book, and we appreciate your support.

INTRODUCTION

Cheltenham Township was one of the earliest surveyed divisions of Philadelphia County. With William Penn's arrival in his province in 1682, the migration of English Quakers commenced in earnest. First purchasers were granted a lot in the city of Philadelphia, as well as a more sizable portion of land in the country. Early Quaker immigrants Tobias Leech and Richard Wall quickly established themselves on their land in what is now Cheltenham Township.

From the beginning, Cheltenham was blessed with the Tookany Creek, the waters of which powered mills, thereby encouraging economic growth. The Tookany Creek begins in Laverock and meanders east through the township before making its way into Philadelphia (as the Tacony Creek) and finally to the Delaware River. In addition to the Tookany Creek, Cheltenham Township also had a variety of early roads connecting meetings, mills, and markets. Old York Road was ordered in 1683 and was laid out as far as Jenkintown by 1692. Limekiln Pike was laid out in 1716, but the lower section dated from an earlier time. Church Road was laid out in 1732, although the section of that road connecting Leech's mill with Germantown dated to 1704. Abington Road (now Washington Lane) connected the Abington and Germantown Meetings and was laid down in the mid-1730s. Another of the early roads ran from Germantown to Lower Dublin (now the Bustleton area of Philadelphia) and traversed portions of Central Avenue and Ashbourne and Oak Lane Roads. This route connected the early mills in Milltown (now Cheltenham Village) with Germantown and Frankford.

Milling was introduced to the area almost as soon as the first inhabitants established themselves, and the earliest villages developed around transport or milling intersections. Shoemakertown grew around the Shoemaker Mill, located on the creek near Old York Road. The village of Harmer Hill developed at the intersection of Limekiln Pike and Church Road, Edge Hill around the tavern that catered to the many travelers on Limekiln Pike and Edge Hill Road, and Milltown around the large number of milling enterprises in that area.

By the beginning of the Industrial Revolution in the early 19th century, there were already many mills and villages in the township. These mills gradually gave way to newer production processes, indicative of the increasing sophistication and specialization of the regional market economy. The Rowland mills (1796), which replaced the earlier Dungworth-Martin mill; the Miles nail slitting mill (1792); the Myers & Ervien fork factory (1848), which incorporated the old Leech gristmill; and the Hammond Mills (1843) were all based on the manufacture of iron and steel products.

As was common throughout the nation, the advent of the railroad initiated dramatic change. The first train through the area ran in 1855 and had stops in Cheltenham Township at Old York Road (later named Ogontz), Chelten Hills, Tacony (later named Abington and now Glenside), and Edge Hill before traveling on to Gwynedd. In 1859, a platform stop was added near Greenwood Avenue and was called Cheltenham, although the name changed to Jenkintown in 1862. Rail service came to the eastern portion of the township following the completion of the Newtown line in 1872. An extension to Fox Chase was built by 1876, with Cheltenham service commencing in 1875.

Just ahead of the railroad was Edward M. Davis, who in 1854 formed the Chelten Hills Land Association, which began to purchase large tracts of farmland in the area of Chelten Hills. One of Davis's earliest clients was Jay Cooke. He also catered to Abraham Barker, John Wanamaker, and several of the Lippincott families.

Although the Civil War interrupted the development of the area, it enriched the history of the township. Davis's mother-in-law was the famous abolitionist Lucretia Mott. Mott lived in Roadside, a house that Davis owned and an important stop on the Underground Railroad. Both Cooke and Davis provided land for Camp William Penn, the nation's largest and Pennsylvania's only training camp for black troops. The war also enriched the pockets of some of the personages who later established lavish residences in Cheltenham Township. Cooke profited greatly by selling government war bonds, and Peter A.B. Widener, a butcher's son, capitalized on his contract to provide mutton to all Union troops within 10 miles of Philadelphia.

Following the war, Davis consolidated his land holdings and developed Camptown (later called LaMott), which became home to many Irish immigrants working in the mills. The community later attracted black people who wanted to live in an area known for its tolerance. Richard J. Dobbins developed Ashbourne shortly thereafter and, in the 1880s, the Beecher and Myer farms were developed into Cheltenham Village. Other developments—such as Wyncote, Ogontz Park, and Glenside—grew around the train stations that carried executives to and from work in Philadelphia. The introduction of the trolley along Old York and Easton Roads in the late 1890s also fueled the demand for suburban housing.

Simultaneous with the development of working- and middle-class suburban communities was the migration of the very wealthy from Philadelphia to country estates. Often beginning as summer residences, the estates evolved not only into year-round homes for the family but also into museums for art and antiques collections, stables for finely bred horses, and gardens and greenhouses featuring the most exotic and rarest of plantings. If ever there was a place in America where the wealthy congregated in a relaxed environment of luxury and lushness, it was in Cheltenham Township around the beginning of 20th century. However, such was not to last.

The time between World War I and the Great Depression marked a turning point in the pattern of development of Cheltenham Township. Schools catering to the wealthy—such as the Cheltenham Military Academy, Miss Marshall's School, and the Ogontz School—either closed or left the township. The township's milling and manufacturing mainstays during the 19th century all went out of business by 1930. Palatial homes like Idro, Menlo Lodge, Elstowe Park, Lindenhurst, Grey Towers, Lyndon, and Sunset were unable to withstand either the death of their builders or the financial woes of the economic downturn. The homes that did not find an institutional purchaser faced the wrecking ball.

The democratic nature of the economic boom after World War II completed the pattern of 20th-century development in Cheltenham. Many of the remaining mansions were demolished. Although many still survive in the context of some institutional capacity, none of the grandest remains as a private residence. Development absorbed not only the manicured estates but also the remaining farms. Laverock, Cedarbrook, and East Elkins Park all sprang from what had been rolling farmland. An increase in religious and ethnic diversity also marked the postwar period for the township, most notably with the movement of many of the large Jewish congregations to the township from North Philadelphia.

The history of Cheltenham Township is both fascinating and rich. It is our hope that this book will not only be one of learning and discovery but also one of pleasure and enjoyment.

—David B. Rowland, President
Old York Road Historical Society

One

CHELTENHAM VILLAGE AND ROWLAND PARK

The 300 block of Jefferson Avenue is shown c. 1900 in a view looking west from Central Avenue toward Elm Avenue. The windmill appears to be at the back of the property facing Central Avenue that belonged to Henry Rowland. The house on the left also faced Central Avenue and was owned by Martha Humes. William Irvin ran a printing press in the basement of 313 Jefferson Avenue, the near side of the twin house on the right. The twin homes were built in 1870.

The Pumpkin House, at 119¹/₂ Jefferson Avenue, was built between 1897 and 1909. George and Rose Schwartz occupied the house in the early years of the century and are pictured with their children, Mary, Rose, and Jenny. The house still stands as a residence.

Robert Wright's hardware store was located at 218 Beecher Avenue in 1931. By 1934 Wright had moved it to 202 Central Avenue (shown), where he operated the business until he sold it to Charles B. Smith and Samuel S. Dugan in 1945. The business later expanded and moved next door in the 1950s where it remained until Smith's death in 1974.

This pre-1916 view looks west from the intersection of Ryers and Beecher Avenues. On the left are the backs of the homes facing Central Avenue, both of which were built c. 1905. These typical homes were located on the old Myers farm tract, which extended from Hasbrook Avenue west to Central Avenue. The Myers tract was divided in 1885, just a few years before the Beecher farm, which extended east to Central Avenue. The whole area was named Cheltenham Village, and although the old Myers land was largely developed by 1927, there were still many open spaces on the Beecher land.

Ernest Rieben operated a drugstore at the northwest corner of Beecher and Central Avenues from 1904 until 1946. From 1923 until April 1924, the first office of the Cheltenham Bank was located in a back room of this store. In the front was a small area for children to shoot marbles. The building later became Barron's Drug Store and is now the Deli Central store.

Richard Hall built his house, Elm Hill, near the southwest corner of Elm and Beecher Avenues soon after he purchased the property in 1690. The original house was enlarged c. 1765. At this time, the borders of the approximately 59-acre property were Laurel, Cottman, and Central Avenues. Joseph Beecher, a wealthy harness maker from Philadelphia, purchased the property c. 1858. In April 1888, Lynford Cuckle bought the house and a small piece of land bordered by Elm, Beecher, and Grove Avenues. The house is still standing.

Lynford Cuckle is pictured on a hay rake on the Beecher farm. Although Cuckle later purchased the Beecher house, the majority of the farm was sold for development. The Real Estate Trust Company purchased 52 acres in April 1888, and the remaining acreage was bought by John A. Green on the same date. The area, along with the Myers farm to the east, was developed as Cheltenham Village.

Graydon, located on Laurel Avenue, was built sometime between 1850 and 1870 and, for more than 40 years, was the home of Richard Penn Lardner. Future owners were George R. Justice and the William B. Gill family. In 1908 it became St. Joseph's Villa, a convent and convalescent home for the Sisters of St. Joseph of Chestnut Hill. It remained such for 60 years. It was enlarged and renovated in 1940 and, in 1968, became known as Sacred Heart Hall, a retreat house and residence for the sisters. In the 1980s it was converted to the offices of United Hospitals Inc., which occupied the property until c. 1999. The Fox Chase Cancer Center is the current owner.

The Rowland School was named for Thomas Rowland. The original four-room school opened in 1915 on the south side of Myrtle Avenue, facing Elm Avenue. In 1924 a six-room addition was built and, in 1964, more rooms were added. The school closed in 1977 because of decreasing enrollment. Now owned by the township, the building is home to the Rowland Community Center and the East Cheltenham Free Library.

The new Methodist church, located on the northeast corner of Central and Myrtle Avenues, was built in 1915 to replace the original structure on the east side of Rowland Avenue, south of Ashbourne Road. On Sunday morning, June 27, 1915, the congregation met for the final time in the old sanctuary. After the service they marched together to the new location. The building was formally dedicated that evening.

Trinity Chapel is located at the northeast corner of Central and Laurel Avenues and was built in 1906 by an Episcopal congregation. In 1924 the chapel became a self-sustaining parish, St. Aidan's, and moved to a new building at Central and Cottman Avenues. The original building then became the home of the Pilgrim Lutheran Congregation until 1955. The building now serves as the house of worship for the New Apostolic Church.

The Cheltenham Hook and Ladder Company No. 1 was formed in September 1896, and the first firehouse was built by December of that year at 514 Ryers Avenue. In 1906 a two-door brick addition was added to the front of the original building. The fire company moved to 413 Ryers Avenue c. 1923. The brick firehouse building is now the office of accountant Gerald Barr.

Men of the Cheltenham Fire Company No. 1 are pictured here with an early horse-drawn wagon. When the fire company received its first automobile pumping truck in 1916, it enlarged the doors and reinforced the floors of the firehouse to accommodate larger, heavier machines.

This *c.* 1903 view of the 500 block of Central Avenue is looking north from Old Soldiers Road toward Laurel Avenue. Mary Laird owned the property at the near right. The Cheltenham Post Office is now on the site. The land on the left was part of the Ames Shovel & Tool Company property and is now the site of public tennis courts.

The W.H. Hoover house, at 512 Ryers Avenue, was built *c.* 1900. It is located north of the firehouse and is now occupied by the Guerin law offices.

Tobias Leech, a Quaker from Cheltenham, England, built this house at the northeast corner of Ryers Avenue and Old Soldiers Road for his grandson Abraham in 1721. The building was sold to Jacob Myers in 1773 and remained in the Myers family until 1917, when it was sold to Francis Taylor, a founder of the Cheltenham Bank. Taylor, a Quaker, erected a meetinghouse on the grounds near his home in 1921. After the Friends moved to Jeanes Hospital grounds in 1956, the meetinghouse became a private home. The Hollinger family purchased the Leech-Myers residence in 1985. It now serves as a home and as offices for Barandon & Hollinger Real Estate.

This view of Old Soldiers Road is looking west from Hasbrook Avenue toward Ryers Avenue. Old Presentation BVM Church is to the right. The parish was founded in 1890 and was the only Roman Catholic parish between Frankford and Jenkintown. The building was designed in 1891 by Edwin Forrest Durang. Materials used in the construction came from Visitation Church at Lehigh and B Avenues in Philadelphia. The congregation built a new church across the street in 1967, and the old building was demolished.

Wagons carrying the materials for the construction of the Ryers Avenue bridge *c.* 1912 pause at the corner of Old Soldiers Road and Hasbrook Avenues. The Cheltenham train station (at that time in Cheltenham) stands to the right. An act of the state legislature in 1915 enabled Philadelphia to annex 84 acres of East Cheltenham, which placed the station within the city limits.

Mary Laird owned this 18th-century house at the northeast corner of Old Soldiers Road and Central Avenue around the beginning of the 20th century. It later served briefly as the second post office of East Cheltenham before the postal service moved into larger quarters at 502 Central Avenue in 1915. The house is now Michael's Appliances.

Archibald McQuilkin came to Cheltenham from Philadelphia in 1894 and established a small grocery business in Cheltenham Hall, shown here. In 1904 he moved the business to the corner of Central and Myrtle Avenues. Previously, Cheltenham Hall had been used by Presentation Church for worship before the church on Old Soldiers Road was built in 1891. The building was demolished prior to 1957, when Drach's Gulf Station was built. The current owner, Tookany Park Auto Service, has occupied the site since 1967.

Albert Myers's store, built in the early 1800s by Charlotte Black, housed the Cheltenham Post Office for nearly 60 years after its establishment in 1855. In 1866 Myers became the second postmaster, serving for nearly 31 years. Myers family descendants owned the store until 1906, when James and John Houldin purchased the building. In 1959 Cheltenham Township acquired the building, which became the home of the East Cheltenham Library until 1977, when the structure was demolished.

Benjamin Rowland bought the old Dungworth Mill in 1795. In 1796 his nephew Benjamin Rowland Jr. bought land downstream near Samuel Miles's nail slitting mill and established a bed screw plant; he later expanded to shovels as well. This was the Lower Mill of the Rowland Mill complex. In 1801 Rowland Jr. purchased some of his uncle's land near Jenkintown Road and established a tilt hammer and blade mill. The elder Rowland retired in 1810. After several different owners, Rowland Jr. acquired the old Dungworth Mill property. His son, Thomas Rowland, took over the business in 1824 on his father's death and consolidated the mills into one company. Thomas's brother Benjamin joined the firm shortly after and, in 1835, two more brothers, William and Harvey, joined. The mill was manufacturing 14,500 shovels a year by 1832. The mills expanded to include the manufacture of saws in 1830 and coach springs by 1842. Steel was added in 1845. By 1860 the company had so many diverse interests that the family decided to dissolve the firm. The brothers left to manufacture steel in other areas; Thomas retained all of the Cheltenham works and concentrated on shovels. In the same year, two of his sons joined the company, and a third became a partner shortly after. Thomas retired in 1871, leaving his three sons in charge of the firm, which was then known as T. Rowland's Sons. In 1888 the mill was destroyed by fire. When rebuilt, the mill was the second largest shovel factory in the United States. In 1901 the Rowland family sold the business to the Ames Shovel & Tool Company, which operated it until 1928. The site was abandoned and eventually demolished. The entire 36-acre mill area became part of Tookany Creek Park. This photograph, looking toward the Central Avenue Bridge, shows the Lower Mill complex.

20

In the 1890s, shovel mill workers worked in the mills five and a half days per week. Hours were from 6:30 a.m. to 5:00 p.m., with a half hour for lunch. Day workers received $1.50 per day. They lived in housing provided by the mills along the Tookany and on nearby streets. Some of these homes still exist.

Two dams supplied the power to the Rowland Mill complex. The upper dam was on a branch of the Tookany Creek near Jenkintown Road and serviced the Upper Mill. It was the more powerful because it was higher. The lower dam, pictured here (and Lower Mill), was located a few hundred feet upstream from where the creek turns south near Central Avenue. The sluice is still in evidence in Tookany Creek Park.

The earliest part of the house known as the Shovel Shop at 300 Ashbourne Road was built in the early 1700s, and the east addition was added c. 1830. Benjamin Rowland Sr. purchased the house when he moved to Cheltenham from Chester County in 1795. It remained in the Rowland family until 1901. The last family to live in the house moved out in 1928 when the shovel works was abandoned.

Cheltenham Township acquired the Shovel Shop in 1934. The building was restored in the 1940s, as pictured, and again in 1976. The building is listed on the Inventory of Historic Places and the National Register of Historic Places. Since the township became the owner, the building has housed a variety of different businesses. It currently houses an investment and financial services firm.

Barth's Bakery was located at 600 Central Avenue and was originally the home of Jacob Barth. The township acquired the building in the early 1930s to be used in conjunction with the Tookany Parkway system. It was later rented and then demolished in the 1980s.

This view looks west on Ashbourne Road toward Rowland Avenue from Central Avenue. The building on the corner was Harry Ott's barbershop. It was built in the 1700s as a residence and later served as a candy store, frequented by many students from the Heller School. It was demolished in 1964 by the township in preparation for the widening of Ashbourne Road.

The Jay Vees Building at 409 Ashbourne Road was originally one in a row of houses built for workers in the Rowland Mill. The frame addition was added at a later date. In 1940 the building became the first home of the Cheltenham Art Center and served as such for 12 years. It then became the headquarters for the Cheltenham Jay Vees and is now used by Boy Scout Troop 321 of Presentation BVM Church.

The Richard Drake house was built in the late 1790s or early 1800s for workers at the shovel mill. Located at 415 Ashbourne Road, Little House has been in the Kochey family since 1930. When the Kocheys bought the house, it had no doors, windows, heat, or light. They worked on improving the home until 1934 before moving in.

In 1795 Benjamin Rowland Sr., Samuel Miles, and Frederick Altemus each gave a part of their land to form a lot big enough to build the first free school in Cheltenham. In 1857 a room was added and the name was changed from Milltown School to Cheltenham School. In 1883 the building was torn down and a new one erected on the site at 439 Ashbourne Road. This school was named the George K. Heller School after a prominent school director and long-term member of the school board. In its earliest years, the Heller School served the first through eighth grades. It later served the first through sixth grades and, by the mid-1900s, only the fourth through the sixth. When Cheltenham Elementary School opened in 1953, the Heller School became home to the Cheltenham Art Center.

The Cheltenham Methodist Church began as the Milltown Methodist Class Meeting and met in homes starting in 1816. Sometime before 1831, it acquired a regular preacher and, in 1845, it built its church on land donated by Thomas Rowland on the east side of Rowland Avenue, between Ashbourne and Highland Roads. An addition was built in 1854. It was the first church in Cheltenham Township. In 1915 the congregation moved to a larger building and, in 1921, the original building was demolished. Behind the church building to the east was the church cemetery. When the church building was demolished in 1921, the cemetery expanded westward into the vacated space. Many early Cheltenham residents are buried here. The church parsonage was located immediately to the south of the church building. The parsonage house is now a private home.

The Order of Red Men, a fraternal organization based upon the customs and antiquities of Native Americans, began in Norristown in 1846 as a patriotic association among men who had volunteered to defend Fort Mifflin in 1813. The Philadelphia Tribe No. 3, the Lenni Lenape, was created very soon afterward. In 1887 the order established a home for its retired members at Ninth and Race Streets in Philadelphia. In 1889 the Philadelphia home moved to the house built *c.* 1870 by Thomas Rowland for his daughter Mary when she married Frank Hansell. It was on the east side of Rowland Avenue, south of Highland Road. In 1914 a 20-bedroom addition was completed. Thirty-five tribes supported the home and, over the years, 400 men lived there. By 1964 there were only four men living in the home, so it was sold and demolished later that year.

The Rowland Mansion was built in the late 1790s by Col. Samuel Miles. It became the property of Judge McKean and then of John C. Cresson, from whom Thomas Rowland purchased it in 1833 and added a wing to each side of the main house. The Rowlands sold the house in 1922. The two wings were removed and the original home was converted to a twin dwelling in 1925. It is located at 817–819 Rowland Avenue, between Croyden and Boyer Roads.

The Curtis Country Club was established by publishing magnate Cyrus H.K. Curtis as a private recreational club for the employees of Curtis Publishing Company. It opened in 1916 and was located on the Tookany Creek Parkway between Front Street and Ashmead Road. There were tennis courts, a swimming pool, baseball and football fields, a track, a clubhouse, and more than 100 bungalows on 155 acres. It became the Melrose Country Club in 1947.

Everard Bolton likely built the original section of the house on the Kerlin Farm, located on the southeast corner of Ashbourne and Oak Lane Roads, shortly after he purchased the ground in 1694. After the American Revolution, the property was known as Pleasant Hill. In 1850 new owners Robert and Margaret Haines called it Heidelberg, and it remained in the Haines family for almost 100 years. Julia and Hugh McLaughlin and Josephine and Alfred Bowker purchased the house and 10 acres in 1944. In 1985 a descendant, Betty Barclay, became the owner. The once beautiful house and the rare plantings are now in great disrepair. This photograph dates from 1885.

Two

MELROSE PARK
AND LAMOTT

Slitting Mill Road, now known as Rowland Avenue, may have been a private toll road for many years. Originally opened to provide access from Ashbourne Road to Samuel Miles's nail slitting mill, the road was extended to the city line through private right-of-way to become an access route to Philadelphia. The house shown here served as the tollhouse on the private road and was located near the present Tookany Creek Parkway and Johns Road. It was most likely demolished during the development of Oak Lane Manor or during the construction of the Tookany Creek Parkway.

The Melrose Carmel Church stands at the northeast corner where New Second Street, Oak Lane Road, and Sunnybrook Avenue intersect. The church was formed in Philadelphia in 1880 and, in 1945, was moved to this site. The building was designed by George D. Savage and built in 1947. This view from the intersection of New Second Street and Sunnybrook Avenue looks east toward Overhill and Brookfield Roads in the mid-1950s; it shows some of the newer homes of that era in the Oak Lane section of the township. This whole area was once part of the 175-acre estate of C.H. Fisher.

The Oak Lane Terrace Improvement Association was organized early in the 20th century and formed its own fire brigade to protect the rapidly developing area. The firehouse was located on Crest Avenue just north of Cheltenham Avenue and is still standing, though much modified. The fire brigade was disbanded around the start of World War I.

Miss Marshall's School was located on the northern portion of the T. Henry Asbury estate and was bounded by Mountain and Valley Roads on the west and north, by Asbury Avenue on the south, and the railroad on the east. The boarding school for young girls was operated by Emma and Mary Marshall and opened in the 1890s. The school closed between 1907 and 1916.

Asbury Lake was created sometime between 1877 and 1891 by damming up a section of the Little Tookany Creek on the estate of T. Henry Asbury. It was located immediately west of the railroad and was bounded on the south by Cheltenham Avenue. The lake was a popular recreational site, providing boating in the summer, ice-skating in the winter, and beautiful landscaped grounds with paths for strolling. The area was increasingly given over to new homes, and, by 1927, the lake was gone and the creek buried.

There was a Melrose station at the western end of Stratford Avenue that was closed when the Oak Lane Station in Philadelphia was relocated to Melrose Park in 1905. For this reason, the Melrose Park Station, located at Mill and Valley Roads and pictured here, was known as the Oak Lane Station as late as the 1970s. The station building was destroyed by fire in April 1979, but trains still use the stop.

These Windsor Avenue homes date from 1930, when the street extended only from Mill Road and Woodlawn Avenue. The north side of the street was originally part of the 70-acre E.T. Schoenberger property, and the south side was subdivided from land belonging to the T. Henry Asbury estate.

The Benjamin Myers Elementary School, located at Montgomery and Union Avenues, was built in 1923 after Montgomery Avenue was extended south through the former Richard Dobbins property. The school served grades one through six from the old Ashbourne School and grades seven and eight in Shoemaker and LaMott Schools. It now houses kindergarten through grade four.

The Ashbourne School, also known as the Union Avenue School, was built in 1872. It served the first through the eighth grades and was also used as the first high school from 1885, when the secondary grades were added one year at a time, until 1906. An addition was built in 1889. The school later housed the Senior High School Industrial Education Department and later became a district maintenance building. It is now a private home.

Richard J. Dobbins, an architect, builder, and large landholder in the Ashbourne area, was primarily responsible for the development of Ashbourne. His estate, Ellerslie, located on the east side of Old York Road between Ashbourne Road and Melrose Avenue, extended east to the railroad. Dobbins bought the land from John Brock, who had purchased it from Samuel T. Leech, a descendant of Tobias Leech. The men shown here are working on one of Dobbins's farms. The estate was divided up piece by piece as the area grew. Although Ellerslie was demolished, the grounds are now the home of Adath Jeshurun and the Mandell Education Campus of the Federation of Jewish Agencies of Philadelphia.

Colony House was Theodore Voorhees's estate, located east of Old York Road with its entrance opposite the intersection of West and Prospect Avenues. It was built in 1907 from the plans of architect Frank Miles Day on land formerly belonging to Richard J. Dobbins. It later became the motherhouse for the Grey Nuns of the Sacred Heart, which operated Melrose Academy on the grounds from 1922 until 1985. In 1987 the Mandell Education Campus took over the property. The house is now the Gutman Early Learning Center.

This *c.* 1922 view, looking north on Old York Road from about Beech Avenue, shows St. John's Lutheran Church, located at the southeast corner of Melrose Avenue. The congregation was established in 1902, and its first building at Stahr Road and Park Avenue in Ogontz was occupied in 1904. In April 1913 the church moved to this new building. In 1964 a Christian education building was constructed. The house to the right was demolished; the lot is currently vacant.

Herman Buchborn's home was located on the northeast corner of Old York and Valley Roads, on the western edge of the E. Clarence Miller property. It was built according to the 1905 design of architect Herbert Clifton Wise, who later designed the garage in 1909 and made alterations and additions to the house in 1916. The grounds featured decorative stone walls, a small lake on the Valley Road side, and entrances from both Old York and Valley Roads. After World War II, lots were subdivided and developed along Valley Road. The building has been converted to professional offices.

Roadside was the home of Lucretia Coffin Mott. Mott, America's greatest abolitionist and an early leader in the suffrage movement for women, moved into the home from Philadelphia with her husband in 1857. The house sat on land purchased in 1854 by her son-in-law Edward M. Davis. The first portion of the house was constructed in 1753, and an addition was built in 1757. The home was a stop on the Underground Railroad. Mott died in 1880 and, in 1888, the settlement of Camptown was renamed LaMott in her honor. Roadside was demolished in 1911 to make way for Latham Park.

William L. Elkins purchased Roadside and eight surrounding acres from Davis. When Elkins died, his estate sold a 28-acre parcel of land to developer William T.B. Roberts. In 1912 Roberts began advertising the prestigious community Latham Park, fronting on Old York Road between Beech and Willow Avenue and extending west to Sycamore Avenue. The name Latham was that of the noble English family from whom Elkins was descended. The exclusive development featured custom homes, each of which was required to cost at least $15,000 to construct (in an age when the average salary was $900 per year). Many of the homes still stand.

36

The LaMott Fire Company was formed in August 1910 by the sons of the early white settlers, and its first piece of equipment was a two-wheeled hosecart that the company stored in a small building at the rear of Willow Avenue and Keenan Street. The first firehouse was built in 1914 at 1618 Willow Avenue and was used until May 1957. The building currently houses a small display on Camp William Penn.

By 1953 the LaMott Fire Company needed more modern quarters. Nathan and Harry Robinson, owners of a portion of the former Widener tract, donated eight acres for a park, and the township commissioners leased a piece of the ground for a new firehouse at Penrose Avenue and Humphrey Merry Way. The new building was dedicated on May 18, 1957.

The LaMott AME Church first began as a Sunday school in the 1880s; later, several members held services in each other's homes. The first church was built in 1888 at 1505 West Cheltenham Avenue from material hauled from the demolition of the Philadelphia Centennial Exposition. White citizens in the area—including the wife of Samuel Clements, the head of the Cheltenham Military Academy, and Rev. Richard Montgomery of Ashbourne Presbyterian Church—helped raise funds. Edward M. Davis donated the land. The growth of the congregation resulted in the construction of a larger building in 1911 on the same site (shown).

As the LaMott AME Church grew over the years, adjacent properties were purchased and renovated to house the various programs of the church. The two houses adjacent to the church were razed when Cheltenham Avenue was widened. Many of the distinguished families in the LaMott community belong to the church.

William Butcher was the first African American to settle in the area of the future LaMott in 1850. He was employed as a tenant farmer by Edward M. Davis and lived in this house at the southeast corner of Willow and Butcher Streets. It is the oldest house in LaMott and is still standing.

Camp William Penn was the nation's largest and Pennsylvania's only training camp for African American troops during the Civil War. The camp was a federal training facility organized and overseen by the Supervisory Committee on Enlistment of Colored Troops. The committee, which included many early Philadelphia Republicans and founders of the Union Club and the Union League of Philadelphia, raised more than $33,000 to finance the training of the regiments. Founded in June 1863, the camp was initially located on property that Jay Cooke donated in Chelten Hills. It quickly outgrew its original space, so Edward M. Davis offered a portion of his property between Sycamore Avenue and Washington Lane for the camp, which then moved. The first recruits arrived in July 1863, and by the time the camp closed on August 14, 1865, a total of 10,940 men in 11 regiments had been trained and sent to serve in the Union army. The regiments were the 3rd, 6th, 8th, 22nd, 24th, 25th, 32nd, 41st, 43rd, 45th, and 127th. Lucretia Mott often preached in the camp, which was adjacent to her home. Camp William Penn contained approximately 50 buildings, including sleeping barracks, a dining area, bathing house, stables, church, school, blacksmith shop, shooting gallery, base hospital, and prison. Following the Civil War, Davis reacquired the land in and around the camp that he had sold in 1854, and he divided it into 50 building lots, which he began to sell in 1867. Thomas Keenan, a carpenter, purchased two acres, which Davis had not been able to secure, and divided the land into six lots. The 30-acre development—roughly bounded by the present-day Willow and Cheltenham Avenues, Keenan Street, and School Lane—was called Camptown, but that name was changed to LaMott in 1888.

Head-Quarters Camp "William Penn,"

CHELTEN HILLS, PA.

FEBRUARY 13TH, 1864

GENERAL ORDER No. 13.

All Visitors to this Camp will require a Pass, to be obtained at these Head-Quarters, or at the Head-Quarters of the Supervisory Committee, No. 1210 Chestnut Street.

By order of

LOUIS WAGNER,

Lieut.-Col. 88th Regt. P.V.

Commanding Post.

GEORGE E. HEATH,

1st Lieut. 6th Regt. U. S. C. T.

Post Adjutant.

HEAD-QUARTERS CAMP "WILLIAM PENN,"

CHELTEN HILLS, PA.

1864

The Bearer, ...

has permission to visit this Camp on ....

....

This Pass Not Transferable, and to be taken up when presented.

By Order of

LOUIS WAGNER,

Lieut.-Col. 88th Regt. P. V.,

Commanding Post.

General Agent Supervisory Committee.

The Supervisory Committee on Enlistment of Colored Troops operated recruiting stations in Philadelphia and interviewed candidates for the camp's officers. Officers were reviewed for their attitudes toward blacks and their knowledge of military tactics. The commander of Camp William Penn was the German-born Col. Louis Wagner, who had enlisted with the 88th Pennsylvania Volunteers in 1861. Wagner had been declared permanently disabled after being wounded at the 1862 Second Battle of Bull Run. When the camp was established, he volunteered for the position of commander and was largely responsible for the camp's success. Although initially there was strong opposition in the city to the enrollment of black troops, early camp successes caused the mood to change. By 1864 Camp William Penn had become a site of wonder and disbelief, and the curious rode out from town to the camp to watch black men drilling and shooting on target.

The first settlers in Camptown were primarily Irish immigrants employed in the nearby mills. African Americans slowly moved into the area beginning in 1850 and, by 1880, numbered 64. Edward M. Davis built the first school in 1868 at his own expense on School Lane. It was a two-room frame building that held 30 students. It was rented to the Cheltenham School District, which bought it in 1870. In 1878 the township purchased a lot at the northwest corner of Sycamore and Willow Avenues and built a stone building for nine grades. There were several alterations and, in 1900, five rooms were added. It later housed grades one through six and, in 1940, was closed. The students then attended the Shoemaker and Myers Schools.

After the LaMott School closed, the township gave the building to LaMott for use as a community center. In 1967 the township took back ownership of the building. It currently serves as a community center and home to the LaMott Library.

42

Three

CHELTEN HILLS

Oasis was the 15-acre estate of William Frederick Fray and was located between Juniper and Beech Avenues on Old York Road. The house was built before 1877. There was a sunken garden between the house and the road, along a stream that ran through the property. John B. Stetson bought Oasis sometime before his death in 1906. The house was demolished when most of the Stetson land holdings along Old York Road were developed for residential housing in the 1940s and early 1950s.

Idro was the summer home of hat manufacturer John Batterson Stetson. It was located on the west side of Old York Road north of Juniper Avenue, with entrances from both streets. Stetson built the house in the 1880s on land he had purchased from R.J. Dobbins. Following Stetson's death in 1906, Stetson's widow moved to a different part of the township, although she maintained the house until the late 1930s. After futile attempts to sell and then give away the elaborate interior woodwork, the house was razed.

Idro was built in the French Chateau style, and the name was from the Russian word for "cool and pleasant." Stetson enlarged the house several times so that the L-shaped building was eventually 120 feet across the front and 120 feet long. He added his own power plant to provide steam heating and electricity. A large open terrace surrounded most of the house.

Idro's large entry hall, which measured 32 by 40 feet, was surrounded by a gallery on the second story with several corridors leading off of it. The house contained a music room and gymnasium. There was an organ on the first floor. Stetson also built a library 29 by 33 feet long extending the full length of the south side of the house.

Stetson was very interested in horticulture and maintained large greenhouses both at Idro and in Florida, where he spent his winters. This greenhouse was east of the house on a rise and housed tropical plants. The grounds also featured two rose houses, a stable, a pigeon house, many winding roads and walkways, and a large lake.

John B. Stetson bought Pleasant Valley from John F. Peniston between 1877 and 1891 for his son G. Henry Stetson. It was still the home of Helen Lewis Stetson at the time of her death in January 1982. It was later demolished for residential development. The estate grounds had been developed previously in the 1950s.

Rhylon, the estate of Henry H. Roelofs, was located at the southwest corner of Old York and Ashbourne Roads. A house was already on the site when Roelofs bought the property in the 1880s and had William E. Dobbins design a new residence in 1886. The extensive grounds were noted for their beautiful lawns and rhododendrons. Stetson bought the property before his death in 1906. The house was demolished in the 1940s to make way for residential development.

Pen-Mar is located on the northwest corner of Old York and Ashbourne Roads. In 1893 it was the home of J.H. Larzalere, but Dr. J. Frederick Herbert purchased it sometime before 1896. Herbert, a prominent civic leader, replaced George Widener on the Cheltenham Board of Commissioners after Widener was lost on the *Titanic*. The house still stands, although the property was subdivided, with the back portion being developed in the late 1920s and early 1930s.

The Webb home, Menlo Lodge, was located on a 17^1/$_2$-acre estate bounded by Cedar Lane and Ashbourne Road, with an access drive from Spring Avenue. The estate was originally seven and a half acres and had been owned in 1891 by W. Fred Snyder, who called it Abend-Ruh. By 1896 William L. Elkins had purchased the estate and renamed it Menlo Lodge. In 1906 Charles J. Webb purchased the estate in its larger size. The year following Webb's death in 1930, the main house was demolished.

47

William L. Elkins bought John Michener's estate, just south of Ashbourne Road with access from Juniper Road. In 1887 Elkins hired architect Angus S. Wade to remodel the house. Work was completed in 1888, and Elkins named his summer house the Needles. In 1892 stables were added to the estate and, in 1894, alterations and additions as designed by William Bleddyn Powell were made to the house. By 1897 the grounds extended from Ashbourne Road to Beech Avenue and Sycamore to Willow Avenues. This photograph dates from August 22, 1896.

In 1898 Elkins demolished the Needles and began construction on a grand Italian-style villa, designed by Horace Trumbauer. The mansion, completed in 1902, was named Elstowe Park. After Elkins's death in 1903, his land holdings were divided. The family retained Elstowe until the Dominican Sisters purchased the house and surrounding land in 1932 after what had been a long period of neglect. The order began using the house in 1933 for retreats and days of prayer, primarily for women. A dormitory wing was added in 1961. The house still serves as the main retreat house for the order.

Elstowe Manor was an architectural masterpiece that housed the Elkins family collection of fine and decorative arts and antiques. The center interior court was an open room 31 feet high with a balcony supported by huge marble columns. The music room was executed in the style of Louis XVI, and the library was oak paneled, with a ceiling said to be a copy of one at a French chateau. The Elkins art collection was ultimately given to the Philadelphia Museum of Art, and the library was given to the Free Library of Philadelphia. Although the furnishings were disposed of after the Elkins family left, Elstowe still retains most of its interior architectural features.

Chelten House, designed by Horace Trumbauer in 1896, was the home of William Elkins's son George W. Elkins. It still stands at the southeast corner of Penrose Avenue and Ashbourne Road. In 1909 a fire damaged the interior portion of the center of the house, which was rebuilt according to Trumbauer design. The Dominican Sisters purchased the property in 1949 from the Stephano family, renamed the building St. Dominic's Hall, and currently use it in conjunction with their retreat house.

49

The original Linwood Hall was built in 1860 for a Mr. Bates. He never occupied the house and, in 1861, Miss Carr, at the encouragement of Jay Cooke, rented the property and established a ladies' seminary. Miss Carr's Seminary remained for a few years and then moved to Eildon. A Dr. L.S. Pepper then purchased the property and, later, Charles Richardson owned it. In the 1880s, Peter A.B. Widener bought the property and began to remodel the house.

Architect Angus S. Wade was responsible for changes to Widener's Lynnewood Hall, as Linwood Hall was renamed. By 1890 there was a new roof, new porches, gables, dormer windows, stone chimneys, a three-story addition, and new outbuildings. The interior featured wood paneling, stone frescoes, new baths, and a modern electric system. It had become the epitome of the latest and grandest Queen Anne–style home. The house was Widener's summer residence.

With the rapid growth of his art collection (which strained the capacity of his mansion on North Broad Street), Widener decided to build anew. In 1898 he commissioned Horace Trumbauer to build a residence that would house his art collection and family. Constructed between 1898 and 1900, the new Lynnewood Hall was patterned after Prior Park in Bath, England. This photograph, taken in 1900, shows the western facade of the monumental residence. The front wings housed the Widener family, and the back wing was reserved for the art collection. In 1910 the Van Dyck gallery was added to the rear of the back wing. The old summer residence was demolished when the new building was completed.

Widener's original art gallery ran the length of the rear wing of the building and was modeled on the European gallery, with paintings hung floor-to-ceiling. After P.A.B. Widener's death in 1915, his only surviving son, Joseph E., refined the art collection, reducing the 500 paintings to roughly 100. He kept only the finest works while adding other masterpieces. The long gallery was redesigned into a series of connecting rooms, which were open to the public for some 25 years during the summer months. As he and his father had planned, Joseph gave the art collection to the nation in 1942 shortly before his death. The Widener collection constitutes part of the core collection of the National Gallery of Art in Washington, D.C.

Cheltenham Military Academy opened in 1871 in Ivy Green, an old mansion in Ogontz. By 1877 the school had moved to this building on the southeast corner of Washington Lane and Ashbourne Road. The founder, Rev. Samuel Clements, died in 1889 and was succeeded by Calvin Rice, who died in 1910, and then by John D. Skilton. Peter A.B. Widener bought the land and demolished the building after the school's closing around the start of World War I. Lynnewood School was built on the corner site in 1951, and today the building houses the school district administration.

Students at the Cheltenham Military Academy included Jesse Grant, Pres. Ulysses S. Grant's son. The school emphasized a wholesome social, moral, and religious attitude among its college preparatory students. Military drill and discipline were also a important parts of the school's daily routine. Daily morning and evening prayers and Sunday evening services were conducted in the school chapel. Students attended Sunday morning services at St. Paul's Episcopal or Ashbourne Presbyterian Churches.

In 1892 George Vaux Cresson commissioned architect Frank Miles Day and Harry Kent Day to design a home to replace the former residence of Edward Mellor, which he had recently purchased. Cresson's 16-acre estate, Caversham, was located at the northeast corner of Washington Lane and Ashbourne Road. In 1904 Joseph M. Steele, one of the region's preeminent commercial and industrial construction builders, bought Caversham and added electricity and phone service to the house before moving in. After his father's death in 1908, Steele separated the eastern section of the estate to build a home, Ballanraes, for his mother and sister.

Caversham included stables, greenhouses, and a large formal garden. The driveway curved up from Ashbourne Road to the porte-cochere, and a large terrace enhanced the front and south elevations of the house. Fitz Eugene Dixon bought Caversham and Ballanraes in 1921 and, sometime between 1927 and 1938, had the Caversham house demolished. Both properties were incorporated into his estate Ronaele. When the Christian Brothers purchased Ronaele, Ballanraes was renamed Benilde Hall. The building was razed to make way for the Homes of Elkins Park development.

In 1861 Jay Cooke founded Jay Cooke & Company, which became a leading banking house in Philadelphia. During the Civil War, Cooke was the U.S. Treasury's fiscal agent. He planned and executed a masterful advertising campaign to sell bonds in small issues directly to the people, the first campaign of its type and a model for comparable fund drives in later wars. On the day the war ended, Cooke broke ground for Ogontz, which was completed in 1867. The 52-room house sat amid 200 acres of land bounded by Washington Lane and Church and Ashbourne Roads. The estate was named after an Ottawa Native American chief well known in Cooke's hometown of Sandusky, Ohio. In 1870 Cooke sought to raise funds for the Northern Pacific Railroad. The spectacular failure of his company through overexpansion and other errors precipitated the panic of 1873. That year, Cooke closed Ogontz and sold its contents.

In 1882 Cooke invited Mary L. Bonney and Harriete A. Dellaye to move their Chestnut Street Seminary to Ogontz, and the school became the Ogontz School. Founded in 1850, the school was a finishing school for wealthy young ladies. The English language was a specialty subject, with Anglo-Saxon and early English as part of the course of study. Theater productions were also an important part of the education, as was poetry and music. Miss Bennett's literature class is pictured at rapt attention in 1893.

The Ogontz School program of physical and mental development included military drill exercises and athletic activities. A gymnasium was located in a separate building north of the main house. Taken in 1893, this photograph of the Ogontz baseball team includes, from left to right, Adele Farrell, Katherine Skinner, Jean Tritch, Gussie Brown, Fannie Heppelfinger, Mary Peavey, Margaret Ogden, and Louise Stetson.

This 1891 view shows one of the ladies' dorm rooms. The Ogontz School was purchased in 1912 by then principal Abby A. Sutherland. The school remained on the Cheltenham property until 1917, when it moved to Abington. The school ground had been purchased in 1915 by Joseph Widener. The house was demolished shortly after the school moved to make way for a new house, Ronaele, the future home of Widener's niece Eleanor and her husband, Fitz Eugene Dixon.

Ronaele was built in 1923 as the home of Eleanor and Fitz Eugene Dixon. The house, designed by Horace Trumbauer, was located on the site of the former Ogontz, which had been demolished. The estate included greenhouses, a swimming pool, a garage, servants' quarters (in addition to an eight-room butler's cottage), and an agricultural and cattle building. In 1950 the Christian Brothers bought the property for their student Brothers attending LaSalle College, and the house was renamed Anselm Hall. The Brothers sold the property for development in 1973 and, after a battle by preservationists, the house was demolished in 1974.

Rock Lane follows a looping course from Washington Lane to Church Road and was in existence by 1877, although known previously as Summit Lane. This photograph shows the house at 869 Rock Lane, which still stands although the road bed has been greatly altered. The view looks south toward the southern intersection with Serpentine Lane. Some of the houses along Rock Lane were demolished when Rock Creek Park was created to relieve flooding problems from the Tookany Creek. The original site of Jay Cooke's mausoleum was nearby.

Four

ELKINS PARK

St. Paul's Episcopal Church held its first services in private homes, although a Sunday school was in existence prior to 1860. The cornerstone for the building at the northeast corner of Ashbourne and Old York Roads was laid in September 1860, and the sanctuary was dedicated in May 1861. Jay Cooke, the great Civil War financier, was a founding member and is buried in the cemetery behind the church. Rev. Robert J. Parvin was the first rector. The rectory was built in 1866–1867, the bell tower in 1869–1870, and the south transept added in 1882. The interior was modified several times. Among the stained-glass windows, the church has 13 windows from the Tiffany Studios dating from 1895 to 1928, two of which were installed as memorials for the Widener family members lost on the *Titanic*.

This late-1800s view of Ashbourne Road looks west toward Old York Road. The white building on the right is Parvin Hall, which belonged to St. Paul's Episcopal Church. It was built by Jay Cooke for use as a parish hall and for the men's Bible class. After Cooke's death in 1905, the congregation replaced Parvin Hall with a more permanent memorial to Cooke. Memorial Hall, now called Jay Cooke Hall, is a stone building that remains in use today. The stone steps at the far right belong to the next property to the east, Chestnutwood.

This house, first known as Chestnutwood, was the property of the wife of Jay Cooke Jr. in 1877. It is located immediately to the east of St. Paul's Episcopal Church, at 509 Ashbourne Road. By 1891 it had become the home of Joseph P. Truitt. By 1909 the back part of the lot had been sold. The front portion of the three and a half acres was the property of Constantino Stephano, and the house became popularly known as the Greek House. Stephano heirs still owned the site in 1937. It is now the Wordsworth Academy.

Ashbourne Presbyterian Church was organized in 1878 and first occupied a building on the north side of Ashbourne Road at Montgomery Avenue. In 1884 the congregation moved to this stone building designed by architect Isaac Pursell, at 323 Ashbourne Road, a little east of their old home. In 1920 an addition was built to the rear. The church moved to Abington in 1965 and became the Elkins Park Presbyterian Church. The Descent of the Holy Ghost Romanian Orthodox Church bought the building and still occupies the site.

Ogontz Park was developed *c.* 1900 by W.T.B. Roberts. This view, looking west toward Old York Road, shows the Spring and Elkins Avenues intersection. The homes were typical of the houses going up near the new Elkins Park Station. Many of them were designed by prominent architects for the well-to-do and still stand today.

The tollhouse at the northeast corner of Old York Road and Spring Avenue was built c. 1896 to replace an earlier house (farther north at Old York and Church Roads) that had become dilapidated. The tollhouse was built to appear as a gatehouse for the Tudor mansion next to it. It was torn down after the road was freed in 1918. The site has been partially covered by later road widening.

Eildon was located at the northwest corner of Spring Avenue and Old York Road. For a time, the estate was home to Miss Carr's Seminary after the school left Linwood Hall. In 1878 Charles Dennis Barney, a banker and son-in-law of Jay Cooke, purchased the estate. Around 1881 the house burned; a Queen Anne–style house designed by Isaac Harding Hobbs replaced the former building. After Cooke's financial reverses, he came to live here with Barney. Eildon was demolished in 1947 and the Elkins Park House was built on the site in 1956–1957.

The William Taylor Blake Roberts residence was on the southeast corner of Old York Road and Elkins Avenue and was designed by Charles Barton Keen and Frank Mead. Roberts, who built most of residential Glenside and developed both Latham and Ogontz Parks, bought the property sometime between 1897 and 1909 and demolished an old house that had previously been on the site. After Roberts's death in 1936, the house was purchased by a Mr. Whitaker, who owned it for a number of years. In 1962 the Greek Orthodox Church of the Annunciation bought the property and moved its Philadelphia congregation to the site. The house was demolished in 1970, but the church incorporated some of the old arched windows in their new sanctuary.

Shifra became the home of Gabriel and Ralph Blum sometime after the brothers married two daughters of Jacob Loeb (in June and September 1891, respectively). At that time, it was the home of Mrs. Jacob Loeb, even though her husband's estate retained ownership of the French Renaissance–style house. The house, built of Trenton brownstone, was built in the 1880s and sat on 59 acres on the west side of Old York Road at the railroad. By 1916 W.T.B. Roberts's Ogontz Land Management Company had acquired the land for development. The house was demolished after the late 1920s. Chelten Hills Drive, Widener Road, and Elkins Avenue now cut through the property.

After the middle of January 1895, trolleys began running up and down Old York Road to Cheltenham, joining the railroad in adding to the transportation boom that brought more and more people to the township. This view, looking north from near Elkins Avenue, shows two trolleys near the railroad bridge.

The original Old York Road Station was built shortly after rail service came through Shoemakertown in 1855. It was located in the extreme northeast corner of the Loeb estate near Old York Road. The name was changed to Ogontz Station in 1888. After the new Elkins Park Station was built in 1899, the older station became the Ogontz freight station. The Chelten Hills Railroad Club, founded in 1946 in Germantown, has rented the building since 1961.

This early-20th-century view, looking north from the railroad bridge toward Church Road, shows Old York Road. The coal yard, which operated for many years under several different owners, is at the southeast corner of Old York and Stahr Roads. It was the home of the Lehigh Fuel Company at the time it was destroyed by fire in February 1980.

The Ogontz Fire Company was organized in 1892 and chartered in 1908. In 1922 the group reorganized after an eight-year period of inactivity. The company stored its truck in the township garage and met at 8036 Old York Road. In February 1925, the company moved into its first real home (pictured here) at 8010 Old York Road, opposite Stahr Road, where it remained until May 1953.

The Old York Road Auction Room was located on the west side of the street between the railroad and Church Road. Some of these buildings were gradually replaced by more modern commercial buildings, and the whole site was replaced when Elkins Park Square was built in 1979.

The Cheltenham Coach Works was founded by William Moore in 1870 and, by 1884, was owned by his son George W. Moore. The company, fronting on the east side of Old York Road between Stahr and Church Roads, manufactured wagons, carriages, and buggies. In 1892 Moore took John Ervien in as a partner, and the company became Moore & Ervien. The business remained in operation until the early 1900s. An addition was later put onto the front of the building that housed the Elkins Park Post Office until 1959 and was demolished shortly thereafter. The main building was demolished in 1970 during the Ogontz Urban Renewal Project.

The Ogontz Hotel was located on the southeast corner of Old York and Church Roads. Licensed in 1856 after the railroad came through, it was the first public house in the township. The building had been there much earlier; prior to it being a hotel, Richard Martin, a tanner, lived and worked there, his tannery stretching down to the creek. Martin also owned a large farm that extended south on Old York Road as far as Ashbourne Road. The building was razed in 1970 as part of the Ogontz Urban Renewal Project.

At the time of this 1913 photograph of Old York Road looking north from Forest Avenue, Old York Road curved to the west along the present Church Road and then curved northeast again to the top of the hill (along the route of the current Old York Road Spur). Trolleys on some of the routes turned around at this point by entering Forest Avenue at the right and pulling onto a loop track to come back to Old York Road. The small shed was replaced by a two-story building. The house behind the shed had been the residence of Richard Shoemaker from 1805 until 1846. The large building in the rear was the powerhouse.

The Philadelphia Rapid Transit Company operated the Ogontz Power House to provide electric power for the trolleys from 1895 to 1940. The building was something of a showcase, with a Spanish tile roof and interior walls of ceramic tile. The equipment was imported from Germany. The trolleys stopped running in September 1940, and the building was demolished in the mid-1940s when the Old York Road was straightened.

In the mid-1940s, work commenced to eliminate the steep hill and curve of the old route of Old York Road. Starting at the current intersection of Church and Old York Roads, the new course was cut north, through the hill, to rejoin the original road at the top, and the whole road was widened. The new Philadelphia Electric Company power plant, built on part of the foundation of the old trolley powerhouse, is clearly shown at the left center of the photograph. Forest Avenue remained as it was.

The Triangle Building was originally a waiting room for trolley passengers located at the intersection of Old York Road and Forest Avenue. It became a tavern and was torn down during the Ogontz Urban Renewal Project demolition work in 1969–1970. Forest Avenue was rerouted to enter Old York Road farther north. The Cheltenham Township Municipal Building, dedicated in 1976, is now at the site.

The Shoemaker Mill was established in 1746 by Dorothy Shoemaker, Richard Mather, and John Tyson. It was located on the south side of Old York Road, opposite the present Old York Road Spur. The Shoemaker family operated it until 1847, when Charles Bosler, a mill employee, purchased it.

The Bosler family operated the Cheltenham Flour Mill from 1847 until it ceased operation in 1923. They remodeled the building and, in the 1890s, converted to steam power, thereby doubling the production of flour. The building was demolished in 1927, and the land is now part of the Cheltenham Park System.

The second permanent home of the Ogontz Fire Company was at 8110 Old York Road from 1953 until the third home at 8215 Old York Road was built in 1980. The day after the company moved to its new location, the service station located next to the old firehouse burned.

The earliest part of Richard Wall's home was built soon after he and his wife arrived in 1682. It was located on the south side of Old York Road and Church Road, near the Shoemaker-Bosler mill. Wall was a Quaker, and the first meetings of the future Abington Friends Meeting took place in his house. It became the Bosler home in 1847 and was named the Ivy. The township bought the property in 1932. Up until c. 1978, when the last inhabitant moved out, it was the oldest continuously inhabited house in Pennsylvania. The township's historical commission now maintains the property as a house museum.

Trolley service as far as Jenkintown began in the middle of January 1895, so this photograph (taken during the winter of 1894–1895) is of a very early trolley car laboring up the old Ogontz Hill, on Old York Road north of Elkins Park (the present Spur) through very deep snow. The house on the height at the left is Berthellyn, the home of George S. Fox.

In 1915 ice-cream manufacturer Henry W. Breyer Jr. bought land adjacent to and south of the John Wanamaker estate at the southwest corner of Old York Road and Township Line. Breyer built his own new home, Haredith (the back of which is shown here), on the west side of Old York Road opposite Foxcroft Road. The house was designed by architect William F. Koelle. The mansion became the township administration building in 1957.

Caleb Fox's home, Natlehigh, sat side by side at the top of Ogontz Hill with his brother Frederick Morton Fox's home, Foxholm. These two houses and George S. Fox's house, Berthellyn, were part of the Caleb Fox estate when they were demolished during the 1944–1946 cut-through construction for Old York Road. Furness, Evans & Company designed all three houses in 1888. This photograph dates from August 1896.

Beth Sholom Synagogue moved to Cheltenham from the Logan section of Philadelphia, purchasing the land on which the Caleb Fox estate had been located. The Conservative Jewish congregation began construction on this building in 1950 and, after it was completed, held services alternately in Logan and Cheltenham. In 1953 the congregation commissioned architect Frank Lloyd Wright to build a new temple, which was dedicated in 1959. It was Wright's last project before his death. The building pictured is now the Fischman Memorial Auditorium.

John Wanamaker bought 77 acres of land bounded by Washington Lane and Township Line and Old York Roads on which he built Lindenhurst in 1883. There were entrances from both Old York Road and the Chelten Hills Station, which the department store magnate later used as his private station. The house, with its many cupolas, piazzas, and various roofs, was an outstanding example of Queen Anne architecture at its most ornate. It housed a very large collection of priceless works of art. There was an artificial lake on the grounds and beautiful gardens. The original Isaac Mather mill, still located in the corner of the property on the Tookany Creek, furnished power to the estate.

In 1907 fire completely destroyed John Wanamaker's first house, along with much of his valuable art collection. The works that were saved were stored in a building that was also destroyed by fire a few months later.

John Wanamaker's son Rodman supervised the building of his father's magnificent new French Renaissance–style home, which, while not as ornate as its predecessor, was much more massive. After Wanamaker's death in 1922, the house was neglected and remained vacant even after Henry W. Breyer Jr. bought the land and house in January 1929. In 1944 Breyer donated the Wanamaker land, along with some of his own, to the Boy Scouts of America, and the house was demolished the same year. The land was developed in the mid-1980s, and the Briar House condominiums and the Pennsylvania College of Optometry are now on the site.

Juliana's Cave, located on Wanamaker's property, was one of many that lined the rocky edges of the Tookany Creek in the Chelten Hills area. This one was a favorite haunt of neighboring children.

The St. James Roman Catholic parish was established in 1923. Its first home was a rented hall on Stahr Road. Later that year, the parish bought a house at Cadwalader Avenue and Waring Road. In 1923–1924, the parish built a school, designed by Francis Ferdinand Durang, which had an auditorium and small chapel, with classrooms on the top floor. This building served as the church. A convent and rectory were added in 1956. A new church at 8230 Brookside Avenue was not built until 1967–1968. The photograph dates from January 30, 1930, and features the St. James Church Players rehearsing for a dramatic production. The ladies are, from left to right, Catherine Breckenreed, Elizabeth Muldoon, Catherine Morrissey, Ann Kenny, Molly Plunkett, Nellie Donahue, Frances Lynch, Catherine Gormley, Ann Harkins, Cecilia Harkins, Nora Byrne, Rita Harkins, and Margaret Murphy.

Rolling Hill, the Walther mansion, sat on a 33-acre site at Township Line and Church and Jenkintown Roads. The house was a stone and plaster Southern Colonial–style building, and the estate included a garage and stable building, a two-story cottage, a swimming pool, and extensive and beautifully planted grounds. The property became the home of Rolling Hill Hospital in 1953, and the mansion served as the early hospital building. In 1989 the mansion was demolished as part of a hospital renovation and expansion program. The hospital is now known as the Elkins Park Hospital of Tenet Health Systems.

John Ashmead, born in England in 1648, purchased the grant for his land from William Penn. Although there is some question as to when the house was built, the original part was probably built by 1705 by Thomas Ashmead. In 1761 William Thomson (Thompson) bought the land, with the then much enlarged house and outbuildings, and it remained in the family until *c.* 1920. Eventually Fitz Eugene Dixon bought the house. Following his death, his son sold the property to its current owners in June 1983. It is located on New Second Street north of Church Road.

The Hammond Mills, established by Charles Hammond in 1843 as C. Hammond & Son, manufactured edge tools and was also known as the Tacony Edge Tool Works. It was located at the junction of Church Road and New Second Street. It was in business until the late 1920s. In 1930 M.L. Blumenthal, an illustrator for the *Saturday Evening Post*, converted the main building to a private home, which it remains to this day.

The Myers & Ervien fork factory was located on both sides of Mill Road at Church Road. It was founded by Jacob Myers c. 1848. In addition to newer buildings, it also used the old Jacob Leech gristmill on the site, which had been built before 1751. The mill remained in business until the early 1900s. In 1915 Smith, Kline, & French opened a chemical dye plant on the site, but the plant was destroyed in a large fire the next year.

Myers & Ervien workers hold samples of the products that the company was renowned for manufacturing. There were 50 employees in 1884. The factory by this time was producing a wide variety of forks and also potato and manure hooks. Many of the old houses for the mill workers still stand along Mill Road.

76

The house of Hester and Tobias Leech stood on the south side of Church Road between Mill and High School Roads. The first house was built shortly after the Leeches arrived from England in 1682. Their grant from William Penn consisted of 600 acres. On part of it, Leech established a gristmill, tanning yard, and an oven for baking sea biscuits. The house burned c. 1700, and Leech had to petition the commonwealth to prove ownership before rebuilding, since all of his documents were destroyed in the fire. During the Revolutionary War, the house was used as a cracker bakery. The house later fell into disrepair and was torn down c. 1923. A row of twin homes now occupies the site.

Part of this house at 371 Church Road dates from soon after Leech arrived in the area. The original house served as slave quarters for the Leech household. Leech used the house as temporary quarters when his home burned in 1700. By 1767 it was owned by the Shoemaker family and, during the latter part of the 19th century, by the Myers family. The Victorian porch addition was removed in 1991, and the house remains a private residence.

The Old York Road Fire Company of Cheltenham building at 7818 Montgomery Avenue was built in 1905, a year after the group received its charter. The company had been founded because the private Ashbourne Improvement Association Fire Company, founded in 1892, could no longer handle the demands of the rapidly growing area. The company was first popularly referred to as the Millionaire Fire Company because of its many wealthy members and the ease with which it raised its operating funds. The building was designed by the architectural firm of Duhring, Okie, & Ziegler, and the rear addition was designed by Stanley Yocum in 1914.

In 1926 the Old York Road Fire Company of Cheltenham changed its name to the Elkins Park Fire Company because of the need to clarify which of the growing communities it served. The company members are shown in front of the building in 1949. The company is still at the same location.

The Elkins Park Station was opened in 1899. William L. Elkins had the station built, and it remains in operation today. The facility was "the handsomest and most complete station on the Philadelphia & Reading Railway with the exception of the Terminal" and was used as a lure for potential buyers in the Ogontz Park Development being built by W.T.B. Roberts on part of the Elkins estate. There were 74 local and express trains a day, with a 21-minute ride to the Reading Terminal; the fare was 10¢. The communities of Ogontz (formerly Shoemakertown) and the northern section of Ashbourne were renamed Elkins Park in 1903.

The Cheltenham High School building on Montgomery Avenue and High School Road was built in 1905–1906 to accommodate the growing number of high school students. The building, festooned for a Fourth of July celebration, is shown here in an early photograph. The township had been gradually adding secondary grades since 1885, a year after the high school was formally organized. In 1927 a new building, designed by architect William Pope Barney, was added immediately adjacent to the old school to handle the expanding school needs. In 1937 a gymnasium building was added. The complex became Ogontz Junior High School in 1959 when the senior high moved to Rices Mill Road. In 1977 Beth Jacob, a Jewish school, purchased the site. The original building was destroyed by fire in January 1994. In 1995 the three structures were razed and the land was dedicated as High School Park.

The Cheltenham Police Department was organized in February 1903 after Cheltenham became a first-class township in March 1900. Its first home dates from 1909 and was located in the township offices on Church Road, just east of Old York Road, opposite Ervien Lane. The original building was just the left half of the one shown here, with the right half added later. In 1957 the township offices moved to the old Breyer home and, in 1958, the Elkins Park Library was established in this building. After the library moved to its present location in 1981, the building was demolished.

The Shoemaker School, built in 1860, was located on the south side of Church Road just east of Old York Road. It was the first public school in the area and was known as the Shoemakerstown School. In 1890 the school moved directly across Church Road to a new building, shown here. In 1909, a large addition was added and the name was changed to honor Robert Shoemaker, a longtime school board member. The school was closed in 1973 and demolished in 1979 to make way for the Elkins Park Library building, which opened in 1981.

Five

WYNCOTE AND CEDARBROOK

This photograph of Washington Lane looking toward Jenkintown is dated April 1958, just before work began to widen the road and to build a new bridge over Chelten Hills Drive. The house on the right was at the corner of Serpentine Lane and was demolished during the widening. It was also necessary at that time to straighten the road, correcting a small bend that had been put in the original route in 1800 by Isaac Mather to enable him to have access to his mill. The high viaduct over Chelten Hills Drive opened in December 1958.

Joseph Mather married into the Russell family in 1697, and it was through his descendants that the original Penn land grant to John Russell passed. His three grandsons, Bartholomew, Isaac, and Benjamin, each inherited a third of the land. Isaac Mather received the eastern portion, bounded on three sides by Township Line Road, Washington Lane, and Old York Road. The house was built *c.* 1769. When Washington Lane was straightened in 1958, the new route put the Mather home on the opposite side of the street from their land. The structure was demolished *c.* 1962 to make way for the Wyncote House Pool and Cabana Club.

A later Isaac Mather, shown here on the occasion of his 100th birthday with his son Israel, was the great-great-grandson of Joseph Mather. Isaac was born on October 27, 1806, and died on November 23, 1907. He had been president of the Abington Library Society Board for 53 years and only resigned as he neared the age of 100.

The Orchard was the home of Daniel B. Wentz during the early part of the 20th century. The house, built in 1840, still stands at 8113 Washington Lane. It was previously owned by Edward Starr (1891) and by Mrs. C. Emma Harrs (1897). By 1937 it was the property of J.L. Jones III.

The Nicholas house is set well back from the road at the southwest corner of Church Road and Washington Lane. It is now the home of Wyncote Academy, founded in 1973. It was the home of the Nicholas family in the early 1950s. Mrs. Nicholas was the sister of Isaac Jarrett, and the land had previously been part of the Lippincott family land holdings.

The Heacock sisters, Eliza, Gaynor, Annie, Jane, and Martha, opened the first Chelten Hills School in 1857 in the family home on what is now Heacock Lane. The Heacock farm extended from Washington Lane along the railroad as far as Fernbrook Avenue. This photograph is from that year and is reputed to be the third oldest photograph taken in the United States. The students are, from left to right, Isaac Potts Mather, Joseph Heacock, Tacie Tyson, Gaynor Heacock, Anna Satterthwaite Williams, Elizabeth Williams Townsend, Hanna Rowland Richardson, Martha Ellen Shoemaker, and Martha Potts Mather. The school lasted about three years and left no records.

Elizabeth Heacock, sister-in-law of the Heacock sisters, opened her own school in 1878 at the urging of her prominent neighbors in Chelten Hills. This school also began in the old homestead, but in 1881 a new house was built facing the newly opened Glenside Avenue near Mather Avenue (now Heacock Lane). The school grew quickly, and Annie Heacock joined her sister-in-law as coprincipal. It was called Chelten Hills Select School and used both the old house and the much enlarged newer house. In 1891 another building on Heacock Lane was opened (shown here). The school closed in 1902.

1912

3 cylinder Chase chain driven Truck.

Billy Green at the wheel

This 1912 photograph of the Montgomery County Ice and Cold Storage Company shows Billy Green at the wheel of a three-cylinder, chain-driven truck belonging to the J. Howard Hay painting company. The ice company was located on Glenside Avenue opposite Webster Avenue, and J. Howard Hay was on Greenwood Avenue east of Fernwood Avenue. The building was demolished and the site is now at the western end of the Edward Hicks Parry Bird Sanctuary, which runs along Chelten Hills Drive.

The water from this dam on the Tookany Creek near the Jenkintown train station fed the Mather mill, which stood at the point where Washington Lane crosses the creek. This area is now covered partly by station parking and partly by a small Cheltenham Township park. The dam was torn down when the park was established. It was about 50 feet above the Greenwood Avenue bridge.

This photograph from January 8, 1898, shows a primitive part of Glenside Avenue looking west toward Greenwood Avenue. The partially obscured dark building second from the right is the Case store. Of the buildings along Greenwood Avenue, only the second from the left still stands. It was designed in 1895 by Joseph Linden Heacock for James F. Walsh and is now the Greenwood Deli Market.

The C.M. Case store, located at Greenwood and Glenside Avenues, is shown c. 1900. It was built c. 1893 for James Nile and may have been designed by Horace Trumbauer. Shortly thereafter, the building was the J.E. Luskin store and, after 1897, became the C.M. Case store. Its appearance was altered over the years and, in 1935, the building was demolished to be replaced by a service station. In 1968 the building to its left was razed for the expansion of the service station.

The Jenkintown Light Company, founded in 1890, was the first electric light company in the area. The first office was housed in a building at the corner of Greenwood and Glenside Avenues. In this c. 1905 photograph, Howard Colby is on the left and William Davis is next to him. The company office remained at this location until c. 1907, when it moved to West Avenue in Jenkintown. In 1909 the company lost its identity when it began the series of consolidations that eventually made it part of the Philadelphia Electric Company system.

The Benson Iron Works were housed in a c. 1900 building on Greenwood Avenue opposite Fernbrook Avenue. The company manufactured ornamental ironwork, and its products were used in many of the large homes in the area. This photograph dates from 1947. The building is one of three that were purchased by the Zaslow brothers in 1979 and completely renovated for use as offices for their company, ADT.

These are some of the new homes that were built in Wyncote in the 1890s. The lower homes are at 152 and 156 Greenwood Avenue, and the upper ones on Fernbrook Avenue. This photograph dates from 1893.

When the Harmer Hill School moved in 1853, Wyncote was the only community in the township without a public school. To meet this need, the township rented space in Mrs. Perry Smith's home at the southwest corner of Greenwood and Fernbrook Avenues. The first class was held on September 17, 1894, with 37 pupils and Florence Ridpath as teacher. Students attended this school for only one year, before moving to the newly built Wyncote School, three blocks west on Greenwood Avenue.

Ezra Loomis Pound, American poet and critic, was born in Idaho in 1885 but came with his family to Philadelphia, then to Jenkintown, and finally to Wyncote by 1891. The family lived in this house at 166 Fernbrook Avenue. He attended the Chelten Hills School from 1891 to 1893, then the Wyncote Elementary School, until enrolling at Cheltenham Military Academy at the age of 12. After he began living in a dorm at the University of Pennsylvania, he rarely returned to this house, which remained his parents' home until auctioned in 1930. Beginning in 1908, Pound lived in Europe, moving from London to Paris and, by the early 1920s, to Italy, where he settled. Pound's prose and poetry had a tremendous effect on the literary generation of his time. His fascist sympathies and anti-American views forced him to live in exile in Italy until his death in 1972.

The Wyncote Men's Club was formed in 1906 and held regular meetings in the Parish House of All Hallows Episcopal Church. The purpose of the organization was "the promotion of good fellowship, sociability and interest in Church work generally." Monthly meetings provided a speaker or some other form of entertainment and refreshments. Gradually members began to be more interested in civic and local interests. The name of the club was changed to the Wyncote Civic Association when women were admitted in 1992.

89

Taken on December 5, 1897, this view looks down Bent Road toward All Hallows Episcopal Church. The church was started as a mission of the Church of Our Savior in Jenkintown in 1891 and was known as St. Paul's Mission. A small frame building was constructed and used for the first time on Easter Sunday 1892. The name was changed to All Hallows by the time the first church building, designed by Frank Furness, was completed in 1897. The rectory was built in 1909 on a design by the firm of Thomas, Churchman, & Molitor, and the parish house was built in 1926, designed in the Tudor Revival style by Frank R. Watson.

Calvary Chapel, originally the Wyncote Mission, was formed in 1891 as an offshoot of Grace Presbyterian Church of Jenkintown. A wooden chapel was built and opened on Easter Sunday 1891 on the southeast corner of Fernbrook and Greenwood Avenues. In September 1892, the building was moved (at a cost of $185) to a larger lot on Bent Road directly opposite the home of Henry Walt and immediately adjacent to All Hallows. Construction began on a permanent church in the spring of 1898. The building was designed by Dull and Peterson, and was formally dedicated in May 1899. Alterations and additions were made to the building in 1927 on plans of George Espie Savage.

Friday
Nov. 9
1934

WYNCOTE PLAYERS

Curtain
at
8:30

"AREN'T WE ALL".

By FREDERICK LONSDALE

A COMEDY IN THREE ACTS

Presented under the Direction of
A. RAYMOND BISHOP
and
FRANCES M. WARREN

CAST—IN ORDER OF APPEARANCE

Morton	J. Henry Warren
Hon. Willie Tatham	William D. Scattergood
Lady Frinton	Ethel M. Lutz
Arthur Wells	Louis Standish
Martin Steel	Robert E. Parent
Kitty Lake	Helen E. Rorer
Lord Grenham	A. Raymond Bishop
Margot Tatham	Ruth Wood Carnwath
Hon. Mrs. Ernest Lynton	Mary Elizabeth Nash
Rev. Ernest Lynton	Herbert Johnson
Jacob Willcocks	Francis P. McKenney

Presented By Special Arrangement with
Samuel French, Inc., New York

The Wyncote Players were organized in 1930 at All Hallows Church. Roger Haydock was the first president, and the initial meetings were held in his home. The amateur group produced various plays each year and received wide public praise for its productions. The group was exclusive, and formal dances followed the performances. After World War II, the group became more democratic and expanded to producing six shows each season. In the early 1980s, the group moved to Abington Friends School in hopes of becoming a regional theater but shortly thereafter ceased operation.

William H. Berger built his home, Fairview, sometime between 1877 and 1891 on a rolling hillside at Fernbrook and Maple Avenues. In 1928 he gave the home to the German Reformed Church. Over the years, the building has been engulfed by the expansion of the Wyncote Church Home retirement community.

Bend Terrace is the name of the home that Henry K. Walt, president of the Jenkintown Trust Company, bought from William C. Cochran in the early 1890s. The house, at 301 Bent Road, sat on a nine-acre property bounded by Greenwood Avenue, Bent Road, and Walt Lane. It was built in a French-Normandy style by Cochran c. 1892 to a design by Horace Trumbauer and featured a massive elevated stone veranda. There were spectacular views over the beautifully landscaped grounds, which included a small lake on the Greenwood Avenue side. The estate was broken up and sold in several parcels c. 1980. Cheltenham Township eventually bought a large portion of the grounds and dedicated Robinson Park in October 1995. The house is still standing.

RES. OF W. C. KENT, WYNCOTE, PA.

Nangeomar was built by William C. Kent II on Bent Road in 1907 on eight acres that he purchased from H.W. Cramp. He named the house for his three children, Anna (Nan), George, and Marjorie. In 1909 Kent became the first rector's warden of All Hallows Church, and the church cloister was built in his memory.

The Wyncote Public School was opened on September 2, 1895. The building, located at the southwest corner of Greenwood Avenue and Walt Lane, replaced the temporary school in the Smith home three blocks east on Greenwood Avenue. It remained open until 1948, when the current school was opened at Rices Mill and Church Roads. The building is now used for professional offices.

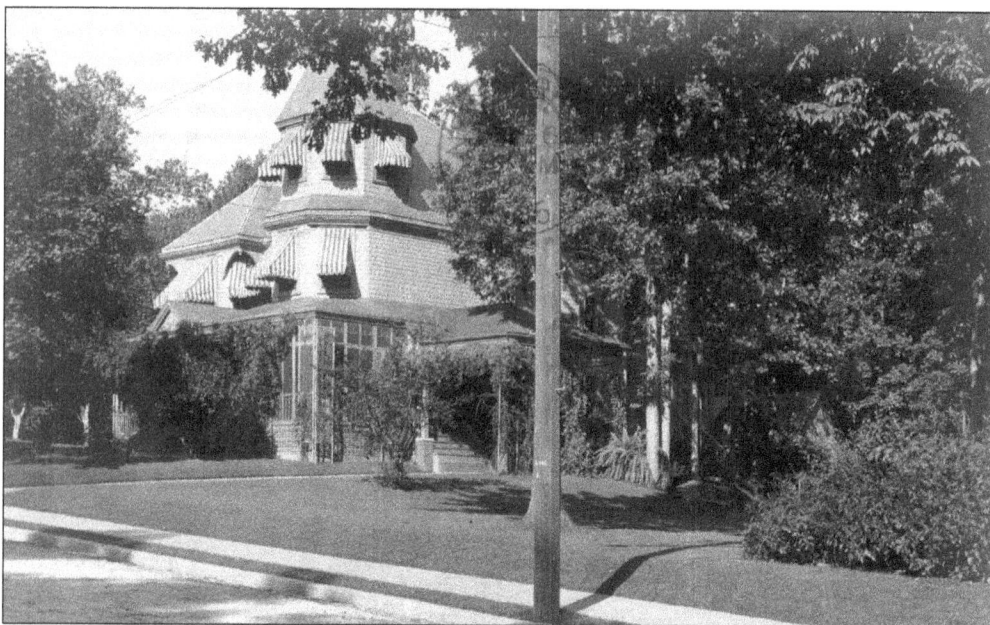

The first development in Wyncote was on Woodland Road where five summer homes were built in 1885 by Willis P. Hazard, and other homes soon followed as new streets were opened up. Oakshade, located at 127 Woodland Road, was built in 1894 for Josiah Kendall Proctor, one of the founders of Proctor & Schwartz, a machinery manufacturer. The house still stands.

The Thomas Williams Junior High School was built on Hewett Road in 1928. The building was demolished in 1970 and the site is now the Thomas Williams Park.

Dunluce, the Scottish word meaning "light on the hill," was located on Greenwood Avenue opposite Walt Lane. The mansion was built c. 1900 by Col. John I. Rogers, the first owner of the Philadelphia Athletics. In 1917 Max Sladkin, manufacturer of the Black Beauty Bicycle and the Ace Motorcycle, purchased the property. He maintained a ranch of silver foxes on the property. The house was demolished in the 1950s.

Hedgely was built in 1896 for Joseph Corbit Davis, an iron and steel manufacturer. The property was later owned by Andres Kaas, a jeweler in Philadelphia. It was during Kaas' ownership that Mark Twain was entertained to dinner here. A fire greatly damaged the house in 1914, and it was later owned by Howard Eckels. Designed by Mantle Fielding, the house is one of the few remaining homes in eastern Montgomery County designed by him. The property, located on Wyncote Lane, now Deaver Road, was subdivided in 1948 and again in 1965, but the house remains.

The pumping station at North and Paxson Avenues belonged to the Jenkintown Water Company. Founded in 1889, the water company drilled a 350-foot well in Wyncote and maintained two standpipes next to its office in Jenkintown. A man with a flag standing on top of the high standpipe signaled the pumping station when the water level needed to be raised. The pumping station was located near the railroad tracks behind the present SGS Paper Products Company. The building still stands and is currently the home of Mack Electric Devices Inc. This photograph dates from 1897.

The Harry Prock Cabinet Company, founded in 1930, was located at 1 Rices Mill Road from 1933 until 1955. The building was sold to Standard Pressed Steel and became Plant No. 3, which ran through 1966. Central Safety Company later occupied the building for a time. SGS Paper Products Company, founded in 1977, moved into the vacant building in 1980.

This mill was built by Isaac Knight in 1725. It was owned in 1877 by Daniel R. Rice, who called it the Green Bank Flour Mill. This 1880 view shows the original building. It was located at the northeast corner of Rices Mill Road and Glenside Avenue.

Daniel Rice enlarged his mill building by adding a second story and new roof, shown here in 1897. In 1901, W. John Stevens converted the building to a carpentry mill. The shops at Glenside Plaza are presently located on the mill site.

In 1866 Abraham Barker, a prominent banker and financier, built a mansion on his property on the southeast corner of Greenwood Avenue and Church Road. In 1890 Barker's firm suffered severe financial losses and he had to give up the house, named Lyndon. Cyrus H.K. Curtis first rented the house in 1891 and bought the property shortly thereafter. In 1895 Curtis hired the architect William Lloyd Baily to design a new residence. In June of that year, demolition of the old mansion commenced. A new Lyndon, built at the cost of $2 million, arose in its place. In 1903 Curtis added a music room to the house. Curtis, seen sitting in the chair to the right, was founder of the Curtis Publishing Company, which published the enormously successful *Ladies' Home Journal* and (beginning in 1897, as a result of an acquisition) the *Saturday Evening Post*. Curtis continued to acquire adjacent land over the years; by the time of his death, the estate totaled 170 acres.

After Curtis's death in 1933, his publishing empire began a slow decline. In 1937 his daughter Mary Louise Curtis Bok sold off a large portion of the estate for development and hired architect Erling Pedersen to oversee the demolition of the house, with the retention of the music room and potting shed. She then offered the property to the township free of charge. In this view of the southern facade of Lyndon, the music room is the structure to the left.

After the death of Mary Louise Curtis Bok Zimbalist in 1970, Curtis heirs sued the township to regain the acreage she had given the township. At this point, it was discovered that the gift of the property was only good for her lifetime, not in perpetuity. The township was able to purchase one heir's half after his death but could not reach an agreement for the remainder. The township finally condemned the property in 1974 and negotiated a cash settlement, thereby retaining 47 acres of ground. The property is now the Curtis Arboretum.

Milmoral, located on the south side of Church Road opposite Accomac Road, is a Georgian Revival–style house that was built for Horace Fetterolf by his brother Archibald in 1902 on land that he had purchased from Isaac Shoemaker. The stable was added in 1905 and a library in 1912. The John P. Nissens purchased the property in 1943 and, upon Mrs. Nissen's death in 1997, the property was given to the National Trust for Historic Preservation, which recently sold it to a private owner.

Cyrus Curtis built a home for his stepdaughter and her new husband, John C. Martin, in 1924 on the northeast corner of Church Road and Greenwood Avenue. It was designed by Horace Trumbauer and was a brick Georgian residence. After the Martins left c. 1947, the building housed Notre Dame High School for girls for eight years. It was bought by the Ritter Finance Company in 1955 for use as its headquarters. The company added a large but architecturally sensitive extension to the back of the house. The Reconstructionist Rabbinical College, founded in 1968, moved into the building in 1982.

The Gribbel estate, St. Austel Hall, was located at the northwest corner of Rices Mill and Church Roads. The house was built in 1900 for gas meter manufacturer John Gribbel and was altered twice. The grounds included two stables, greenhouses, and a 1905 Tudor-Elizabethan addition that combined cottages with auto houses. In this aerial photograph, Rices Mill Road runs along the right and Church Road along the bottom.

St. Austel Hall's main entrance drive curved in from Church Road to and around this porte-cochere on the east side of the mansion. It then continued around the house to garages in the back and to the other outbuildings. The house was designed by Horace Trumbauer in the Cotswold style of the English home of William Morris. The property was cleared for development in the early 1950s.

Belgraeme was the estate of George Horace Lorimer, whom Cyrus Curtis hired as editor of the *Saturday Evening Post*. Lorimer bought the house shortly after he moved to Cheltenham in 1895. The 22-room house is located on the north side of Church Road, west of St. Austel Hall. The building is now the home of the Handmaids of the Sacred Heart of Jesus, who purchased it in 1945 for use as their Ancillae-Assumpta Academy.

Endsmeet Farm was owned by Anna Wharton Morris by 1891 and contained 110 acres bounded by Church and Rices Mill Roads and Limekiln Pike. The land had belonged to Joseph S. Lovering in 1877. The house was located near the present Carleton Avenue. In 1955 the property was condemned by the School District of Cheltenham Township, and the building was razed for the construction of the new high school.

Cheltenham Senior High School opened in 1959 on a 50-acre tract just off Limekiln Pike and Rices Mill Road; it was hailed as having "school buildings as modern as a jet plane and just as sleek." The school cost $6,390,000 and had 54 extra-large classrooms, an Olympic-size swimming pool, a 10,000-volume library, a 1,200-seat auditorium, and a 1,600-seat gymnasium. It is still in use and is currently undergoing renovations.

The Fenton family held several pieces of land near the intersection of Greenwood Avenue, Rices Mill Road, and Limekiln Pike. This house on the estate of James Fenton belonged to Francis Fenton from c. 1877 to c. 1897 and was located north of where Rices Mill and Greenwood now come together. The entrance was from Limekiln Pike. By 1909 the house belonged to Alice H. Baltzel. Homes built in the 1930s are now on the site.

This 1959 aerial view looks from Philadelphia northwest across Cheltenham Avenue toward the new Gimbels Department Store branch that opened in 1955 between Washington Lane and Limekiln Pike. In 1960 a series of small stores was added to the east, extending to Washington Lane. This view clearly shows the residential development that was continuing in the area, including the Lynnewood Gardens complex, shown here on the east side of Washington Lane.

The Cedarbrook Country Club was formed in 1920 by members of the Stenton Golf Club of Philadelphia, whose former home had been sold for building lots. The members converted an old farm on Limekiln Pike north of Cheltenham Avenue, using two barns for the clubhouse. The club moved to Blue Bell in 1952, and the site became the Cedarbrook Hill Country Club, with membership restricted to residents of the Cedarbrook Hill Apartments.

Six

GLENSIDE, EDGE HILL, AND LAVEROCK

The ground for Holy Sepulchre Cemetery was purchased gradually over a span of years from several different owners. Archbishop Patrick Ryan purchased the original 50-acre tract of land at the northwest corner of Easton Road and Cheltenham Avenue in 1892. The first burial was in 1894. Additional tracts were added in 1893, 1897, 1910, 1928, and 1929—the last two purchases made by Cardinal Dennis Dougherty. The cemetery extends along Cheltenham Avenue from Easton to Waverly Roads back to the 309 Expressway and is administered by the Archdiocese of Philadelphia. This 1959 view shows the cemetery and the adjacent construction of the expressway, which was built in the late 1950s and early 1960s.

In 1881 William Welsh Harrison, president of the Franklin Sugar Refining Company, purchased J. Thomas Audenried's farm and country home, Rosedale Hall, at the southwest corner of Church and Easton Roads. After the house burned in January 1893, Harrison commissioned Horace Trumbauer to design his new home. The new residence, known as Grey Towers by the beginning of the 20th century, was inspired by Alnwick Castle in England. The building launched Trumbauer's career as architect to the very wealthy. After Harrison's death in 1927, the estate was sold to Beaver College in 1929. The college continued to use both this campus and their Jenkintown site until 1962, when all operations were moved to Glenside.

Grey Towers contained 41 rooms (excluding servants' quarters), many of which were done in various French styles. The great hall, with its massive barrel-vaulted ceiling, enclosed about one-third of the interior space. The room is in the French Renaissance style with architectural elements imported from Europe. Beaver College uses the building for its administrative offices and many of the rooms retain their original features.

The entrance and gatehouse to Grey Towers, located at the corner of Church Road and Limekiln Pike, were designed by Trumbauer in 1892 as part of the work he did for Harrison prior to the fire that destroyed the main house. The lodge is now called Blake Hall and houses the development office of Beaver College.

Harrison expanded the original Audenried estate into a 183-acre self-sufficient working farm. Trumbauer designed the stables and carriage house complex in 1892 as part of his original work on the property. The building, now known as Murphy Hall, contains art and theater studios and an auditorium.

This 1922 view looks east on Church Road toward the intersection with Limekiln Pike and beyond to the Easton Road bridge. Church Road was laid down in 1736 to connect Trinity Church in Oxford with St. Thomas' Church in Whitemarsh. The house at the northeast corner, one of the last from the village of Harmer Hill, is now gone. The site is a parking lot for the adjacent apartments, which were built in 1961 and are now owned by Beaver College. On the right is the stone entrance gate to Grey Towers.

The No. 6 trolley route went from Philadelphia to Willow Grove. Pictured on its final day of operation in June 1958, the trolley entered Cheltenham Township near Easton Road, crossed Church Road about two blocks east of Easton Road, and then ran through a cut parallel to Bickley Road until it reached Keswick Avenue. The power substation, built in 1904 and now owned by Beaver College, stands on the north side of Church Road where the trolleys crossed the street.

Thomas R. Elcock built his house at the north end of his long, narrow, 10-acre property running from Waverly Road south almost to Church Road on the west side of Limekiln Pike. The house formerly fronted on Waverly Road. The building, which still stands, has been converted into apartments and is owned by the Westminster Theological Seminary. This photograph dates from 1898.

The Glenside Public School was built in 1907 and opened in 1908 on Easton Road north of Springhouse Lane. The building was used as a public school until 1956, when classes were transferred to the present-day Glenside Elementary School on Limekiln Pike. The building was demolished, and a Hess service station now occupies part of the site.

The Samuel Ervin Deihl estate was located on the east side of South Easton Road near the present site of a shopping center and directly across the road from the former Glenside Public School. Diehl was associated with Jay Cooke & Company in the 1870s and with Manufacturers' National Bank in the 1880s. In 1888 Diehl founded a beverage bottler and supply company. He later started Diehl Motor Truck Works, a manufacturer of motor trucks that were used by many bottlers in the eastern part of the country during the 1920s. In 1904 the Diehl family moved to this estate from the Oak Lane section of Philadelphia. In 1907 Diehl purchased two adjoining properties. The four-acre estate extended from Easton Road back to Bickley Road. The house, in the Spanish style with a red tile roof, was destroyed by fire in 1940.

The Diehl dining room is decorated in Victorian splendor.

Bishop McDevitt Catholic High School on Royal Avenue was opened in December 1958, with 750 students. Enrollment hit a high in 1963 with 2,259 students, and later fell after Archbishop Wood High School opened in Warminster, thus removing the Willow Grove area pupils. The McDevitt marching band was organized in 1963 and was chosen in 1979 to escort Pope John Paul II during his visit to Philadelphia. The building is shown from the southeast corner.

The Glenside Free Library was originally located in the Glenside Memorial Hall in 1928. Two years later it moved to a location in Abington Township. After outgrowing various subsequent locations in both Abington and Cheltenham Townships, residents and community leaders recognized the need for a more permanent home. In 1966 construction began on a new building near the southeast corner of Waverly Road and Keswick Avenue. The facility, designed by local architect Leon Clemmer, opened in 1967. Shortly thereafter, the library became part of the Cheltenham Township library system.

W.T.B. Roberts developed most of residential Glenside. These homes were built in 1900 and still stand on Keswick Avenue across from Renninger Park.

Memorial Hall was dedicated on Memorial Day 1927 to the memory of those who served during World War I. On Veteran's Day 1944, the building was rededicated to veterans of all U.S. wars. The building is located on the northeast corner of Waverly Road and Keswick Avenue. In 1968 the building came under township ownership and management.

St. Luke's Chapel was founded in 1905. Its first home was in a small building on Easton Road between Mount Carmel Avenue and the railroad tracks. In 1906 it moved to another site on the west side of Easton Road facing Wesley Avenue. In 1909 the church moved to its present site in Abington Township at Easton Road and Fairhill Avenue. The confirmation class shown here is posing on the steps of the 1906–1909 chapel.

113

The First Baptist Church of Glenside grew out of prayer meetings held at various homes from 1894 to 1900. Regular services began in 1901. When officially organized in 1903, the congregation constructed a building on the northeast corner of Easton Road and Wesley Avenue. The church built a larger sanctuary in 1928 at Waverly and Hewett Roads in Wyncote. The original building was demolished, and the site is now occupied by a bank.

J.S. Phillips Hardware was located on the northeast corner of Easton Road and Wesley Avenue. This photograph dates from 1930. Glenside Hardware now occupies the building.

The Glenside National Bank was chartered and opened for business in February 1910 in a small store at the corner of Glenside Avenue and Bickley Road. Soon after, larger facilities were needed and a new building, as pictured, was built at the southeast corner of Easton Road and Glenside Avenue. The building was designed by the firm of Folsom, Crowe, & Stanton. A few years later, two small wings were added to the rear of the building. It was razed in 1929.

In 1925 the Glenside National Bank merged with the Glenside Title and Trust Company, forming the Glenside Bank and Trust Company. More space was needed, so the original building was razed and a new one was opened in 1929. This photograph shows the interior of the new bank building shortly after opening. The building now houses a branch of the PNC Bank.

The Glenside Pharmacy was located at the northeast corner of Easton Road and Glenside Avenue. This photograph, taken in 1926, shows the original level of Easton Road before construction of the railroad bridge. The Active Tube and Tire Company was next door with a street-side Gulf gasoline pump. The site is now occupied by an H & R Block office.

This 1926 photograph shows the parking that is still located just north of the railroad tracks on Railroad Avenue, but which can no longer be entered from Easton Road. Renninger & Renninger Realtors was located in the building at the right. The Roberts Real Estate building is partially hidden at the back right.

116

In 1856 the North Pennsylvania Railroad first ran a single track through Glenside to Gywnedd. By 1869, a double track was in place and, in 1873, a station was built. The present-day Glenside Station, still in the original building, was first known as the Tacony Station for the creek that ran nearby. The name was soon changed to Abington because of confusion with the Tacony area of Philadelphia. This photograph of Abington Station predates 1888.

In 1888 the name of the station was changed to Glenside at the request of Martin Luther Kohler, who was responsible for the development of the area in the 1880s and who had applied for a post office under the new name. The original railroad crossing at Easton Road is shown from the northeast in 1926.

By 1926 the railroad crossing at Easton Road had become quite dangerous. Therefore, in 1928, the crossing was reconfigured, resulting in the construction of the railroad bridge. This impressive project necessitated the lowering of Easton Road for several blocks both north and south of the actual bridge. The level of the train tracks was not altered.

Trains kept using the tracks and many businesses remained open during the construction project. Looking north toward the east side of Easton Road (toward Mount Carmel Avenue), this view shows a restaurant, the Glenside News, Harry's Meat Market, the National Fruit Company, and the Raiser grocery store.

Temporary sidewalks and scaffolding were rigged in front of the affected businesses in the construction area. Shown just south of the tracks in July 1928 are, from left to right, Moskowitz Brothers, Glenside Market, Holcomb & Furman's former location, the Glenside Trust Company offices, and the Almar Store.

When construction was complete, those buildings still in place needed new fronts and entrances at the former basement level. Stairs gave access to Gunn's Bakery, Rosenberg's Reliable Store, and Renninger Realtors in this building at the southwest corner of Easton Road and Mount Carmel Avenue.

The Glenside Fire Company was organized in 1900. The equipment was stored first in a building at 2262 Mount Carmel Avenue and was then moved to another temporary site at Glenside Avenue and New Street. In 1907 it was moved to the first firehouse (shown here), located on the north side of Glenside Avenue at Lismore Avenue. The wagon carried a leather riveted fire hose, leather water buckets hanging neatly from a rod, lanterns, and soda acid fire extinguishers. The building was remodeled later to add another truck bay where the door is behind the driver.

The Glenside Fire Company moved to a new home about 100 yards away from the old building on Glenside Avenue in 1927. This 1954 view shows the new building with the one-story addition that was completed in 1949. The company was the pioneer in the the United States for establishing an instructional school for volunteer firemen in 1924. The reverse cross on the 1927 building is an ancient symbol of prosperity and good fortune.

In 1943 William Green purchased the McCaughey Mill's lumber, coal, and feed yards south of the railroad tracks and established Primex Garden Center at 435 West Glenside Avenue. Old silos belonging to the former mill can be seen in the back right background in this 1953 photograph, but they were later razed. Primex built a modern building near the street in 1958. In 1981 the old mill building along the tracks was destroyed by fire. The Green family still owns Primex and has modernized and enlarged the business over the years.

David Heist bought a farm in Cheltenham in 1847. The Heist property later grew to include two large farms adjacent to each other along the east side of Limekiln Pike from Glenside Avenue to the junction of Easton Road and Limekiln Pike. Shady Nook Farm was the northern farm, consisting of 59 acres. David's son George inherited the land in 1881. This section of Glenside remained largely undeveloped until after 1916.

This February 2, 1898 photograph looks north on Limekiln Pike toward the intersection with Willow Grove Avenue. The building at the southwest side of Limekiln Pike and Willow Grove Avenue was later owned by the Schmidheiser family. The old Eagle Hotel is just beyond it. The building across Limekiln Pike at the right was either demolished or completely remodeled when the Italianate Schmidheiser building was constructed.

The Eagle Hotel was built in 1710 and stood on the northwest corner of Limekiln Pike and Willow Grove Avenue. The hotel was a major stopping place on the Limekiln Pike, which existed in a very primitive form as early as 1693, and was established as a toll road in 1840. Today the building is the Edge Hill Tavern.

This 1959 photograph looks south on Limekiln Pike toward the intersection with Willow Grove Avenue. The Schmidheiser store on the east side of Limekiln Pike faces Willow Grove Avenue. The building dates from 1873 and housed a feed store when J. Edward Schmidheiser purchased the property in 1955. Schmidheiser continued to sell feed and grain; he gradually added other items, and it became a general hardware store. The building across Limekiln Pike was the Schmidheiser flower store for some years. The store was sold to Ed and June Hinks in July 1978; they retained the Schmidheiser name. The store was sold again in 2000 and now houses an insurance company and a pizza parlor.

The Edge Hill School opened in 1890 and was located on the east side of Limekiln Pike south of Glenside Avenue. One acre of land was purchased from George D. Heist for the building. The school was originally three rooms but was expanded in 1900 to four rooms. Even after the Glenside Public School opened in 1908, the Edge Hill School continued to teach children who lived in the upper part of western Glenside. The school closed in 1940 and, in 1948, the building became the property of the Knights of Columbus, who continue to use it. The photograph shows a class in 1902 on the front steps of the school building.

A great many Italian immigrants were attracted to the Edge Hill section because of the quarry work available in the area. The Edge Hill Quarry began operations in the 1880s and was owned later by Manero Brothers. The current owner is Glasgow Inc. The quarry is located west of Willow Grove Avenue at Limekiln Pike.

Richard Morrey freed his slave Cremona Morrey in 1746 and deeded her the piece of land bounded by Willow Grove Avenue, Limekiln Pike, and Waverly and Church Roads. Cremona's daughter, also named Cremona, married John Montier. Their descendants lived in the area called Guineatown (now Edge Hill) for more than 125 years. The back section of the building shown here is the original house of the Montier family. The name Guineatown came from the small group of African Americans that had settled in the area by the 1760s. The house still stands on Limekiln Pike north of Waverly Road.

Mary Lawn was the home of William H. Kemble, president of the Philadelphia Traction Company. He purchased Stout Hill from the Stout family and built Mary Lawn, located at the northeast corner of Willow Grove Avenue and Church Road. Kemble died in 1891, and shortly after his wife's death in November 1905, the property was sold to J. Frederick Zimmerman, who remained there until at least 1916, renaming the estate Villa Vesta. The homes on Sunset Road were built in the late 1940s after the house was demolished.

William H. Kemble built Sunset across Church Road from the entrance to his estate for his son Clay. Ground for the house was broken in March 1891 and, by April 1892, the house was occupied. James H. Windrim was the architect and John Garber the builder. Clay Kemble sold the property to William C. Gray in 1909. Alfred Harrison purchased the estate in 1917.

Alfred L. Harrison, brother of William Welsh Harrison of Grey Towers, expanded and renovated Sunset based on plans by the architectural firm of Stewardson & Page. Harrison died in 1927, and the house had a minimal staff until Westminster Theological Seminary purchased the mansion along with 17 acres along Church Road in 1937. Westminster was organized in 1929 by several professors and students from Princeton Theological Seminary and was originally located on Pine Street in Philadelphia. The seminary relocated in 1937 and, over the years, has added several additional buildings. The former mansion is used for administrative offices and some dormitory space.

126

Falcon Hill, located at 1777 Willow Grove Avenue, was the residence of John C. Sims, who built the house c. 1890. Isaac T. Starr purchased the estate and renamed it Laverock Hill. Starr hired New York architect Charles A. Platt to remodel the residence and gardens. Famed landscape architect Ellen Shipman designed the garden layout and plantings in 1915. The house and gardens remain in the family and completely intact to this day. The Starr estate included a large portion of farmland on the north side of Willow Grove Avenue that was eventually need for Route 309. The remaining farmland along with the adjoining Newbold and Shubert estates was developed in the 1950s for residential housing.

Across the street from the Starr residence, at 1740 Willow Grove Avenue, was the more modest residence of Charles A. Platt III. The early-19th-century house still stands. In 1915 additions and alterations were made based on plans by Joseph P. Sims of Furness, Evans, & Company. The garden was designed for Platt's wife in 1923 by Sims when he was with the firm of Willing, Sims, & Talbutt.

ACKNOWLEDGMENTS

The Old York Road Historical Society is once again pleased to work with Arcadia Publishing in this second of three books covering the communities of the Old York Road in the eastern portion of Montgomery County. The society's book committee worked hard to compile the photographs and information needed to complete a project of this magnitude. The committee consisted of Russell W. Hammond, Robert M. Harper, Barbara Kotzin, Albert R. Paulbinsky, David B. Rowland, Robert Singer, Beth Trautmann, and Mary Washington. In addition, Mary Washington assisted throughout the project to track down particular images and historical details while Joyce H. Root, society archivist and librarian, was indispensable in her efforts to research and write a sizable portion of the text. We are also grateful to society member Daniel J. McCormick for his assistance.

A project of this scope would not have been successful without the cooperation and support of many people associated with the communities and families of Cheltenham Township. Valuable assistance was provided by the following: Betty Adams, William D. Barker, Jane Beadle, Charis Bowling, Rev. Robert Calvert, Betty Cataldi, William Chambre, Leon Clemmer, John H. Deming Jr., Miriam Einhorn, Leslie and Albert Filemyr, Frederica Foerster, Marie T. Gallagher, Julie Giampa, Lois Ann Glasgow, Richard Gottschalk, Robert L. Gray III, David Green, Linda Gunn, George R. Haines, Bryan Havir, Heinz J. Heinemann, Sister Kathleen Helbig a.c.j., Andrew M. Herman, Jonathan Ingber, Megan Johnson, James J. McCann III, Frank Montgomery, Nancy Jo Myers, Lisa Peters, Donna Plante, Ann Ranieri, Dr. William Reiber, Louise Bers Rose, Ruth Rudd, Darla Schuck, Barry Schwartz, Michael Seneca, Larry Sibley, Robert M. Skaler, Charles E. Sohl Jr., Dorothy L. Spruill, Joan Sunheim, Jack Washington, Robert Whomsley, David Willard, Eileen Zanine, and Edward C. Zwicker IV.

The Old York Road Historical Society is most grateful to those individuals and institutions that loaned images for inclusion in this book. In addition to the various photographic collections of the society, images have come from the following individual and institutional collections: Betty Adams, Archdiocese of Philadelphia, Beaver College, Cheltenham Fire Company, Cheltenham Township Historical Commission, John H. Deming Jr., Fitz Eugene Dixon Jr., Albert J. Filemyr Jr., Glenside Fire Company, Glenside Library, Richard Gottschalk, Robert M. Harper, Andrew M. Herman, Robert E. Hibbert, Dr. Harvey A. Koople, Barbara Kotzin, James J. McCann III, Elizabeth Mikulik, Ogontz Fire Company, Louise Bers Rose, Robert M. Skaler, Norman Triplett, Mr. and Mrs. Jack Washington, and Westminster Theological Seminary.